WHAT'S
ON THE
GRILLE?

CAR BADGES AND MARQUES

MICHAEL BURGESS

AMBERLEY

First published 2022

Amberley Publishing
The Hill, Stroud,
Gloucestershire, GL5 4EP

www.amberley-books.com

ISBN: 978 1 3981 0352 8 (print)
ISBN: 978 1 3981 0353 5 (ebook)

British Library Cataloguing in Publication Data.
A catalogue record for this book is available from the British Library.

Typeset in 10pt on 13pt Celeste.
Typesetting by SJmagic DESIGN SERVICES, India.
Printed in the UK.

Contents

Introduction

The subject of car names, badges, model names, their origins and development has fascinated me for many years. From moments of simple wonder as to how a car manufacturer came to be using a seemingly unrelated insignia to seeing a badge and thinking, 'What make of car is that?' That and wondering what some of the more interesting sounding model names either meant or where they originated from. Feeding this fascination, I have been accumulating pictures and information on the subject for a long time, and you hold the results of that research in in your hands.

Is this a comprehensive guide? Regrettably not, as such a thing would have to be many times the size of this volume and I would probably still miss some. Will it answer a few questions you have been asking yourself for years? I hope so, and hopefully a few more besides.

I have concentrated the bulk of my material on vehicles either available or well known on the UK market, so if you are reading this overseas and I have inadvertently missed out one of your favourites, I apologise.

Bearing in mind that cars have been about for well over a hundred years now, some of the tales of how manufacturers came by their names and badges have become the stuff of myth and legend. Some are obvious, some less so, and some have more than one tale of their origins. In many cases badges and insignias have changed over the years, so I have done my best to track these changes. So read on and hopefully learn a few new things about your favourite cars.

Abarth

Produced: 1949–date.
The Badge: The scorpion of the badge, set on a red and yellow heraldic shield over a lightning bolt, represents the astrological star sign of the company founder Carlo Abarth. The red and yellow background colours were chosen as a tribute to the city of Merano, where his father was born. The lightning bolt behind the shield (later across the top of the shield) has stripes of the colours of the Italian flag. The company name is written across

the top of the shield against a blue field. Early cars have the shield sitting at an angle, later ones have the shield upright.

Carlo Abarth started constructing modified FIAT-based road and racing cars in 1949. In 1971 the business was purchased by FIAT and became a badge used on the sporting versions of FIAT cars, or for sporting upgrade kits for customer's existing vehicles.

AC

Produced: 1907–date.
The Badge: The AC Cars badge is a simple pair of letters curved to the right. Sometimes displayed on the grille, and later as a raised 'AC' badge with the lettering displayed on a round chrome boss. During their associations with the engines of other manufacturers (Bristol was a notable one), the name of the engine manufacturer was sometimes written around the lower edge of the badge.

The 'AC' of the company name stood for 'Auto Carriers', originally a partnership formed between engineer John Weller and butcher John Portwine. Their company was initially known as Autocars and Accessories Ltd, producing three-wheeled vans under the model name 'Autocarrier' for local deliveries. The Auto Carriers name was officially adopted in 1907 when the business moved to Thames Ditton. They would officially become AC Cars in 1922.

Famous AC models would include the Ace (named after the top-ranked playing card as an indication of it being the best) and the 428, named after the capacity of the American V8 engine in cubic inches.

The classic curved AC letters displayed post-war style on a raised boss. The Bristol legend around the bottom of the badge indicates the engine type fitted to the car.

Alfa Romeo

Produced: 1910–date.

The Badge: Alfa Romeo was originally based in Milan, and their badge was inspired by the Visconti family of that city. The family was founded by Umberto, who famously slew a mighty serpent (some describe it as a dragon) that had been roaming the area in the fifth century.

Popular legend has it that the young draughtsman, tasked with designing a badge for the new ALFA cars, was waiting for a tram when he spotted their crest on the wall opposite him. One side depicts the aforementioned serpent devouring a person, while the Christian cross on the other signified the family's involvement in the First Crusade. The draughtsman reversed the two sides of the coat of arms left to right, set them in a circle rather than a shield and the ALFA badge was created. Early versions had the wording 'Alfa' at the top and 'Romeo' at the bottom of the badge, while modern versions have both words written above.

At times 'Milano' has been added to the bottom of the badge, signifying the location of the company, and the whole circular badge surrounded by a winner's garland to signify Alfa Romeo's racing wins.

The ALFA part of the name came first, correctly written at the time as A. L. F. A., standing for Anonima Lombarda Fabbrica Automobili (Association of Lombardy Car Makers). The Romeo part of the name arrived when investor Nicola Romeo took control of the bankrupt company in 1915.

The longest-serving name in the Alfa Romeo range arrived in 1954 in the form of Giulietta. Giulietta is a girl's name (Julia would be the nearest English equivalent), soon joined by the Guilia (little Giulietta).

The Alfa Romeo badge has heraldic origins that stretch back to the Crusades. Some versions would add 'Milano' around the bottom of the badge and a winner's garland.

In 1971, Alfa Romeo introduced the Alfasud (literally Alfa South), so named as it was built in a new factory in southern Italy, constructed as part of a government-sponsored drive to bring employment to the rural areas.

During the 1980s Alfa Romeo produced a Nissan Cherry/Alfasud hybrid in the same factory under the model name ARNA, an acronym that stood for Alfa Romeo Nissan Automobile. Nissan themselves would market it as the Nissan Cherry Europe.

Model names were dropped in favour of numbers during the 1980s; the idiosyncratic 75 model was launched to commemorate seventy-five years of the marque in 1985.

Long-standing lesser badges have included the Quadrifoglio Verde (green four-leaf clover) applied to their performance models and derived from the good luck symbol of racing driver Ugo Sivocci from as far back as 1923. Performance models are regularly badged Veloce (pronounced 'Vel-o-kay', which translates as 'fast', from the same roots of as the word velocity.).

Allard

Produced: 1936–58.
The Badge: Allard cars are best remembered for their exaggerated waterfall-style grilles shaped to resemble the initial letter 'A' of the company name.

Above the grille sat a discrete badge bearing the Allard name in white letters, with an artistic drop shadow set against a red enamel background.

The bold waterfall-style grille, which distinguished all Allards, was designed to resemble the initial 'A' of the marque name. Much more discrete was the dark enamel badge above, which spelled out the name in full.

The company was named after the founder Sydney H. Allard. His V8-powered specials successes in pre-Second World War sporting events led to orders for replicas from other drivers.

In 1945, Allard cars proper was formed and production began, using mainly US army surplus V8 and V12 engines as powerplants.

The naming conventions of the Allard range were simple. There was a model series or mark number (one, two, three, etc.) prefixed by a letter to indicate the body style. J indicated a two-seat sports car; K, a two-seat tourer; L, a four-seat tourer; M, a drophead coupe; and P, a saloon. Thus, a Mk 2 four-seat tourer would be an L2.

Sydney Allard personally drove a P1 saloon to victory in the 1952 Monte Carlo Rally, becoming the only driver to win the rally in a car designed by himself.

When American engine supplies became difficult Allard introduced the smaller Palm Beach (named after the American holiday resort) model with Ford or Jaguar power, and later still the Clipper micro car, named after a sailing ship.

The name had a last gasp in the form of modified Ford Anglias called Allardettes (small Allard) and finally as a supplier and later manufacturer of aftermarket Shorrock supercharger kits.

Alvis

Produced: 1920–67 (cars) and 1920–date (military vehicles).
The Badge: Alvis cars wore a simple red enamel triangle atop their radiator grille with the word 'Alvis' within. When the company ceased car manufacture and the spares department continued to produce parts it was christened 'Red Triangle spares'.

For a time, Alvis made use of the advertising slogan 'The hare ahead of the hounds' and alert-looking hares became a popular after-market mascot on their cars.

Their sporting cars, designed to compete with the likes of Bentley, were the Silver and Crested Eagle, both supplied with suitably imposing avian mascots.

The Alvis red triangle badge lived on after the road cars in the title of the spares organisation 'Red Triangle spares'.

Company founder T. G. John, a former naval architect, named his new car after the engine produced by Aluminium Alloy pistons. Their propriety engine was named Alvis. The exact inspiration for the engine trade name of Alvis is lost in the mists of time, but one theory is that it was made up of parts of two words; the 'AL' of aluminium and 'VIS', which is Latin for 'speed', as typified by the motion of their pistons.

In 1967, after being purchased by Rover, Alvis ceased car production to concentrate on the production of military vehicles, which continues to this day.

Armstrong Siddeley

Produced: 1919–60.
The Badge: Armstrong Siddeley cars were famous for their Sphinx mascot. This was chosen because the company considered it to stand for the qualities they sought in their cars. It was a 'silent, inscrutable symbol of wise perfection'.

Early examples were very accurate, complete down to the now largely eroded headdress and forelegs. In later use on the Sapphire models the Sphinx would sprout wings and jet engines in recognition of the company's successful range of jet engines of the same name.

The name Siddeley entered British motoring in the form of John Davenport Siddeley (later Lord Kenilworth), who designed a car in association with the Wolseley motor company. The Armstrong Siddeley company was formed when the Siddeley-Deasey company merged with the car-making arm of Armstrong-Whitworth, founded by Sir W. G. Armstrong, to form Armstrong Siddeley in 1919.

The early Armstrong Siddeley Sphinx badge faithfully reproduced the forelegs and head dress of the Egyptian original.

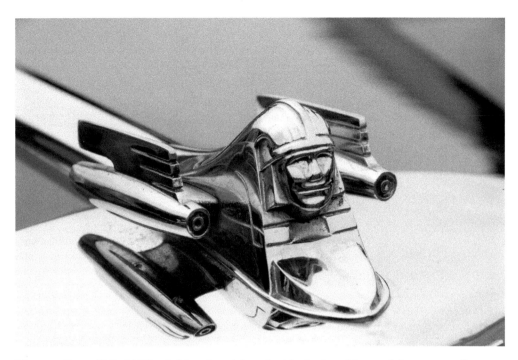

The post-Second World War Sphinx that debuted with the Sapphire model range was far more stylised and sprouted both wings and jet engines in honour of the successful Sapphire range of jet engines.

After the Second World War, Armstong Siddeley claimed to be the first manufacturer to put a new model into production (Healey also claimed this distinction), with a trio of cars named after famous warplanes. There was a saloon called Lancaster, an open tourer called Hurricane and sporting Whitley.

The whole range changed for the 1952 season with the launch of the Sapphire models, named after their Sapphire jet engines.

Car manufacture ceased in 1960 when parent company Hawker-Siddeley merged with Bristol Aeroplanes.

Arnolt

Produced: 1953–58.

The Badge: Arnolt cars wore a heraldic shield, split grey over black, showing Pegasus rising in front of the 'A' initial of the company name. The Arnolt name is written across the middle of the shield. The Pegasus symbolised the thoroughbred rising above the competition.

Arnolt cars were a truly international effort, instigated by Stanley 'Wacky' Arnolt, a Detroit businessman. They had British mechanics (MG, Aston Martin or Bristol), an Italian body with final assembly and painting in the USA.

Largely a US marque, many were sold in Europe and a surprising number of those produced still exist.

The simple Arnolt badge and marque was intended for the American market, but a surprising number of the cars came to Europe and the UK.

Aston Martin

Produced: 1922–date.

The Badge: The Aston Martin name is displayed within a set of geometric wings. While owned by tractor manufacturer David Brown, his name was set above the Aston Martin name within the wings.

The Aston Martin name was assembled from two sources. The 'Martin' part comes from the name of engineer Lionel Martin, who would design their first models. Martin would drive these first cars with some success at the Aston Clinton Hill climb and chose to commemorate his successes in the name of his designs.

The winged Aston Martin badge followed a fashion of the time when the marque was founded. While owned by David Brown his name was displayed above the Aston Martin name.

In 1947, the David Brown gearing and tractor company purchased Aston Martin after answering a newspaper advert offering a car company for sale and inviting offers. He added his initials to all the model names/numbers produced under his ownership (the famous DB Aston Martins), creating a series that would continue (with breaks) to today.

Audi

Produced: 1910–date, but not continuously.
The Badge: The modern Audi badge is made up of four interlocking rings. In 1931, car manufacturers Audi, Horch, DKW and Wanderer amalgamated with an eye to economies of scale to form Auto Union. The interlocked, four-ring badge signified the new links between the amalgamated companies and would come to be the Audi badge when the name was resurrected by the VW group.

The original company to bear the name Audi was founded by Dr August Horch. Horch was already famous for the Horch range of cars that bore his name when he chose to start a second car company in 1910. He named it after a Latin translation of his name. His original company was called Horch Werke, and his second would be called Audi Werke. 'Horch' translates as 'listen' in German, and 'Audi' is the same in Latin.

The best-known model made by Audi was the Quattro, a four-wheel-drive rally car that rewrote the competition car design manual in 1980. Soon every Audi range had a performance version labelled 'quattro' (meaning four), which denoted the four-wheel-drive system.

Audi is perhaps most famous for their advertising slogan 'Vorsprung Durch Technik', which translates as 'advancement through technology'.

Austin

Produced: 1906–89.
The Badge: Austin cars have probably worn a greater variety of badges than any other marque covered here. At the start Austin cars wore the long-lived 'winged wheel' insignia of a single wheel viewed head on with a steering wheel above, flanked by wings and driving through water or dust. It was said to represent rapid, controlled, wheeled motion.

Early versions would be realistic in their depictions while later versions were more art deco in their appearance, with squared-off wings.

The winged wheel stayed with Austin through to the 1950s when it was joined by a flying 'A' bonnet mascot that doubled as a bonnet latch.

From the Austin Atlantic onwards, a version of the Austin family coat of arms sat atop the grille but below the winged wheel, later becoming a circular bonnet badge.

During the 1950s Austin cars had a chrome legend along their bonnet side that proudly proclaimed' 'Austin of England'.

By the 1980s Austin cars were simply wearing the marque name in a square letter style alongside a line of coloured bars of blue and green.

Above left: The original Austin badge of the winged wheel symbolising rapid, controlled wheeled motion.

Above right: The coat of arms of the Austin family would be used as a badge across the whole Austin range during the 1950s and 1960s.

When what had become the Rover group decided to cease using the Austin name the actual lettering was dropped and just the coloured bars remained on the grille of what had been Austin cars.

The company was named after founder Herbert Austin (later Lord Austin). While in Australia Austin would meet and design a car for Frederick Wolseley of the Wolseley sheep-shearing company. They would eventually go their own ways to produce separate ranges of cars, Wolseley eventually coming back under control of Austin after the Second World War.

During the 1950s, Austin models were named after counties or cities in the UK. The big saloons were named after the cities Cambridge and Westminster, while smaller cars were

The phenomenally successful Austin Metro wears the simple last pattern Austin badge used before the name was dropped in 1989.

named after the counties Devon, Dorset, Somerset and Hampshire. A coupe aimed at the American market was named Atlantic after the intended market.

A small four-wheel drive aimed at the Land Rover market was named Gypsy after the intended ability for it to wander wherever it saw fit.

Best remembered of their later models was the small car named Metro (initially the Mini Metro), Metro fittingly translating as 'city' for the intended home of the car.

Austin-Healey and Healey

Produced: 1946–70.

The Badge: The original Healey factory was based in Warwick, and their badge made use of the Warwick crest of the city walls. This was displayed over a Union Jack flag with a Healey banner between the two. The early Healey cars were also distinguished by their upright, kite-shaped radiator grilles.

Later mass-produced Austin-Healey models wore a simpler design of the two names within a winged frame mounted over a compacted depiction of the earlier radiator grille.

The company was founded by and named after famous competition driver and car designer Donald Healey. Post-Second World War, he designed a chassis powered by a Riley engine and named his models after the coachbuilders who supplied the various styles of coachwork. There was Westland, Elliot, Tickford and Abbot. To avoid a purchase tax

Despite their bodies being sourced from a range of coachbuilders, all featured this upright kite-shaped grille. Seen here on a Healey Tickford, named after the suppliers of the body.

Above: The Healey name was joined with Austin when the latter took over the rights to build the Healey 100. Both names were displayed in a simple winged badge.

Left: The original Healey badge made use of the city walls of the town of Warwick where they were based and a patriotic Union Jack flag.

surcharge on vehicles over a certain price, coachbuilders Duncans would produce him a cheap, simple body style.

A road legal racer that used the spare wheel as a rear bumper was named Silverstone after the racing circuit. Unique bodies on a Healey chassis would be shipped less engines to the USA to be locally fitted with a Nash V8 engine and be marketed there as the Nash Healey.

In 1952, Healey adopted the Austin Atlantic engine in a completely new body exhibited at the Motor Show as the Healey 100 (named after the nominal top speed). The production rights were snapped up by Austin and between the press day and first public day the badge was changed from Healey to Austin-Healey and a new marque was born.

Automobile Association

Produced: 1905–date.

The Badge: The AA badge, the symbol displayed by the members of the Automobile Association, has been part of motoring since 1905. The very early badges were in the shape of two interlocked As within a simple circle over a mounting post.

In 1911, the AA merged with the Motor Union, a fellow motoring organisation, and the wings from the top of their badge were added to the top of the simple AA badge. This new badge was registered as a trademark in 1911, and the style many people think of as the classic AA badge had arrived.

The signature of Stenson Cooke, the organisation's secretary, was cast into the shaft of the early badges. Badge No. 1 was issued to the AA chairman, Colonel W. J. Bosworth.

Above left: The first plain brass pattern AA badge. Note the name of Stenson Cooke cast into the mounting shank. He was the AA's first secretary and would write a romanticised account of their founding entitled *This Motoring*.

Above right: The badge of Motor Union, with whom the AA would merge. The wings from their badge would be added to the top of the original pattern AA badge.

Right: A committee member's badge compete with flag. By the time of this later example there is a fixed yellow back plate, the finish is a standard chrome and the signature of Stenson Cooke has been deleted.

The year 1967 saw the introduction of the now familiar, modern-look, square AA badge with two separate letter As on a yellow field, which we still have today.

Committee members were given specially modified badges. On the early style they had a flag attached to the top edge while on the later square type a pair of simple triangular 'wings' were added above the lettering.

Commercial vehicles had their own badges. Initially they were a plain bronze AA badge with a red enamel coating behind the letters, later giving way to a completely chrome badge with a basket-weave pattern backing to the organisation's initials. Following the redesign of 1967 all classes of AA membership used the same square badge.

Bentley

Produced: 1919–date.
The Badge: The 'flying B' is the symbol of Bentley cars. Sometimes it is displayed flat atop the chrome grille, other times it is depicted as a flying B bonnet mascot with wings flying out behind.

On early Bentleys from the original Cricklewood factory the colour background to the 'B' on the radiator badge denoted the state of tune or expected performance of the model. Cars with a black background were 'standard' models while Red label (officially known as the Speed model) cars featured a higher tuned engine. Green label cars (officially the Supersports model) had a shorter wheelbase and engines with a higher state of engine tune again.

Walter Owen Bentley started his company and gave it his name in 1919 but vehicle deliveries did not begin until 1921. These early models were described by their engine size (there was a 3 litre, 4.5 litre, 6.5 litre and an 8 litre) followed by a description of the body,

The Bentley 'flying B' and the winged grille badge have remained unchanged since the earliest days of the marque. Only occasional changes on the background to the grille badge mark out specific models or time periods.

e.g. 3-litre Vanden Plas tourer, the name being that of the coachbuilder who supplied the body. The famous 'Blower' Bentley was officially the '4.5-litre supercharged'.

Later model names would be used such as Mulsanne (named after the longest straight at the Le Mans racing circuit where Bentley had many successes), Hunaudieres (named after a straight at the Sarthe racing circuit), and Brooklands (named after the banked Circuit in the UK, the world's first purpose-built motor racing circuit).

BMW

Produced: 1928–date.
The Badge: The circular BMW badge with the blue and white opposing quarters represents a spinning aeroplane propeller as seen from the front. The imagery was chosen as a suitable badge as BMW were initially famous for their aeroplane engines from 1916. The blue and white colours are taken from the Bavarian flag, the location of the original factory. The letters 'BMW' were added in a bold font above the blue and white symbol.

When the company was founded the name chosen was based purely on the location of the factory, the BMW standing for Bayerische Motoren Werke, which translates as Bavarian Motor Works.

Their first motoring product was a licence-built Austin Seven marketed as the Dixi, a girl's names that means 'popular one'. Their brief foray into micro cars following the Second World War would be badged Isetta, an Italian design from ISO. Isetta translates as 'little ISO'.

Early British imports would be handled by the Frazer Nash company and were badged as Frazer Nash BMW, their name being added to the roundel.

Currently models are badged with numbers. The first indicated the physical size of the car (the higher the number, the larger the car), the latter two the engine size.

The BMW roundel was inspired by the image of a spinning propeller viewed from the front, coloured with the colours of the Bavarian flag. The example here is from a very early UK import by the Frazer Nash company who added their name to the badge. More usually the BMW letters reside at the top of the roundel.

Bristol

Produced: 1947–2011.

The Badge: The coat of arms of the city of Bristol is used as the badge of Bristol Cars. On occasions this was surmounted with the Pegasus symbol of the Bristol Aeroplane Company, their parent company.

Early models displayed the symbol as a round badge with the word Bristol around the top and '2 litre' around the bottom for their early, straight six-engine cars. Later models used a full colour shield of the coat of arms.

Bristol Cars takes their name from the Bristol and Colonial Aeroplane Company, their parent company, which in turn take their name from the city of Bristol where they are based.

Early Bristols were loosely based on pre-Second World War BMW models and Bristol nominally carried on their 400 series of numbers from BMW's 300 series numbers for their early models.

The year 1955 saw Bristol launch the 404, a car that made famous a deeply recessed radiator grille that would become a marque design staple, allegedly modelled on an air vent from the Bristol Brabazon airliner.

Later Bristol models were named after their successful aircraft designs, notably the Blenheim, Beaufighter, Brigand and Britannia.

The coat of arms of the city of Bristol is used as a badge for Bristol Cars. Originally displayed on a round boss with the engine size written around the base, later models such as this use a full colour rendition.

Bugatti

Produced: 1909–date (with gaps).

The Badge: The Bugatti badge is the name in bold white text with a hard black drop shadow to the right set in a red oval at the top of a horseshoe-shaped radiator grille. The initials of the company founder, 'EB', are set above the word 'Bugatti' back to back, so the E is shown reversed in the manner that the company founder signed his initials. The whole oval design is encircled with an oval of red dots – very early versions saw the badge surrounded by red squares.

The company was founded by and named after Ettore Bugatti in 1909 to produce high-performance cars, most commonly seen with French racing blue coachwork. Early models were named in order of production. Thus, the Type 22 was designed before the Type 23 and so on.

Following the death of Ettore in 1947 the business went into receivership and production ceased. The rights to the name passed through the hands of Hispano-Suiza among others and eventually ended up in the hands of VW.

They resurrected the marque name on the modern Veyron, the name translating from Indian as 'Great Man', a tribute to the company founder.

The Bugatti name on the badge is rendered in a remarkably modern drop-shadow lettering style, always at the top of a horseshoe-shaped grille.

Buick

Produced: 1903–date.

The Badge: The Buick marque has had two main badges. After briefly using the simple legend of 'Buick' across a blue and white stripped rectangle, the coat of arms of the Scottish Buick family was adopted. The vertical coat of arms featured a gold stag, top right, and a gold cross with a red gem, bottom left, against a dark red field. A blue and white tartan stripe runs top left to bottom right. This basic form would remain until 1959 when the modern three-shield design was adopted.

The three vertical overlapping shields in red, white and blue for the 1959 season stood for the three new models Buick introduced that year, all three shields still retaining a vestigial remainder of the stag's head and cross of the original badge.

The Buick brand was founded by Scottish David Buick from Arbroath (originally Buik) and it would become one of the original marques that made up General Motors.

Above left: The original Buick badge was derived from the company founder's original Scottish family coat of arms.

Above right: From 1959 the Buick coat of arms would be rendered and simplified on to three shields to commemorate the three models introduced that year.

Cadillac

Produced: 1902–date.

The Badge: The coat of arms badge of Cadillac cars is that of the person after whom the marque was named, Antoine Marquis de la Mothe de Cadillac. Over the years there has been much speculation as to the true identity of de Cadillac, as there are no records of the name prior to him enrolling in the French army. Popular belief has it that he made up his name and noble background to help him get on in the service.

The origins and interpretation of the coat of arms of Cadillac are also a source of debate, but are usually explained thus: the crown at the top of the emblem has seven points or stars, denoting the ancient counts of Tolouse from which Cadillac claimed descent.

The top left and lower right areas of the shield design below the crown display what are commonly referred to as the ducks, appearing three on either side to symbolise the Holy Trinity. Their lack of feet denotes that a Cadillac should not be bothered by earthly things.

One side of the shield denotes the noble lineage of his mother, the other that of his father. The coloured strips in the segments are black (signifying superiority), gold (riches), silver (virtue) and blue (valour). The whole emblem sits above a laurel wreath, which signifies victory.

Cadillac cars started life as the Detroit Automobile Company, then became the Henry Ford Company. When Ford left to start his own company, he took his name with him and the company was renamed Cadillac. This was as a tribute to the founder of Detroit, where the factory was located, and as he was claimed as an ancestor of company founder, Henry Leland.

For a time, in response to the Flying Lady made famous by Rolls-Royce, Cadillac adopted a 'Flying Goddess' bonnet mascot, a female figure with her arms/wings thrown out behind her. Some were realistic figures, while others were more stylised, often featuring glass wings.

The most famous Cadillac model is probably the El Dorado, named after the fabled City of Gold.

Above left: The Cadillac shield has been the subject of intense debate over the years, as has the identity of the man after whom the marque was named.

Above right: In response to the Rolls-Royce Spirit of Ecstasy, Cadillac introduced their own female bonnet mascot in the form of the Flying Goddess.

Chevrolet

Produced: 1911–date.

The Badge: The Chevrolet badge is of an elongated cross design, originally in blue. The earliest versions have the word 'Chevrolet' written across the centre bar of the cross, while modern versions have the shape simply displayed in gold or silver.

Seen in full on more flamboyant 1950s models, the badge has the blue cross mounted against a patriotic red and white shield-shaped design with two French fleurs-de-lis (a French symbol of peace) showing on the red areas lower right and top left.

The cross symbol is allegedly based on design seen in the wallpaper at a hotel where Chevrolet was staying in Paris. Much later the Chevrolet family would claim that he designed the badge himself.

The company was named after the founder Louis Chevrolet. Born in Switzerland in 1878, he moved to the USA and was introduced to Arthur Durant, one time owner of General Motors by Arthur Chevrolet, a relative who worked as his chauffer. Together they formed Chevrolet motors.

The most famous Chevrolet is the sporting Corvette, named after a class of fast ship and wearing a badge of two crossed flags – one the Chevrolet emblem, the other the chequered flag of victory. It had originally been intended to make one of the flags the Stars and Stripes of the United States, but plans had to be changed when they found this was illegal under US law.

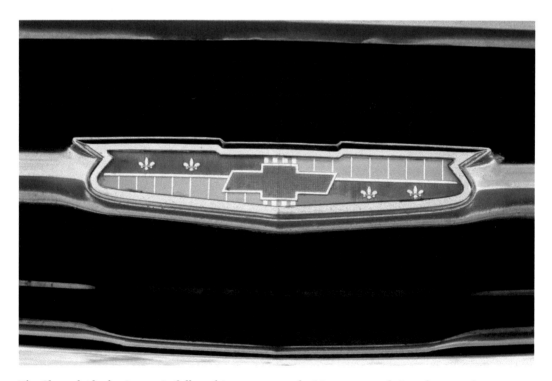

The Chevrolet badge is seen in full on this 1950s example. More commonly just the central cross is used, often depicted in simple chrome on later models.

Chrysler

Produced: 1923–date.

The Badge: In the early days and recently revived, Chrylser displayed the 'Seal of Approval' insignia. This had the Chrysler name emblazoned across a classic 'seal' shape of the type once used on wax sealed documents and was resurrected in 1998.

From the 1960s Chrysler wore what is known as the 'Pentastar' device. Created by designer Robert Stanley, it was said to represent 'something simple, a classic, dynamic but stable shape for a mark that would lend itself to a highly designed, styled product'.

There is a popular interpretation that the five segments of the star represented the five main car brands of the Chrysler group, but Chrysler deny this.

Walter P. Chrysler purchased Maxwell cars and produced the first car to wear his name in 1923. In time, the company would launch or purchase the marques Plymouth, De Soto, Dodge and finally the UK Rootes Group.

Surprisingly for America, UK royalist names such as Imperial and Windsor were used as model names with their own faux heraldic devices as badges.

The Chrysler Seal of Approval was the marque's first badge and has been recently resurrected.

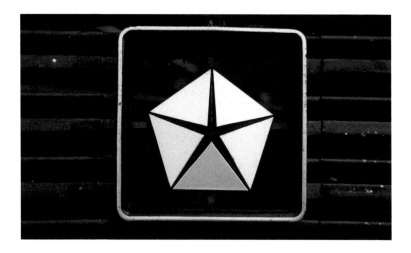

The Pentastar symbol was worn by Chrysler cars from the 1960s until the recent resurrection of their Seal of Approval badge.

Citroen

Produced: 1919–date.

The Badge: The Citroen company started out with the purchase of the rights to produce a revolutionary type of helical gears. The double-peaked Citroen badge represents the unusual teeth arrangement of these gears.

Andre Citroen, after whom the cars were named, graduated from the famous French École Polytechnique and set up in business producing the helical gears he adopted as his company symbol.

The most famous Citroen from the 1930s was the revolutionary Traction Avant (quite literally 'front-wheel drive') range. In the UK it would become known as the Maigret Citroen after the regular appearances in the television serial staring Rupert Davis.

Post-Second World War there was the famous 2CV (2 horsepower) and the far larger DS (Goddess). Later versions of the 2CV would be named Ami (friend) and Dyane (a woman's name translated as being divine or heavenly). In the UK there was a fibreglass-bodied 2CV named Bijou (small and elegant).

The Xsara name, used much later on a large hatchback, is said to represent a feminine person while the Sahara is named after the desert where the Citroen half-tracks made their mark on expeditions between the wars.

The Citroen double arrow grille badge was inspired by the teeth of the Helical gears with which Andre Citroen started his business.

Dacia

Produced: 1966–date.

The Badge: Dacia (Pronounced 'Da-chi-a') wear a simple shield with the marque name across the base. Currently displayed as a simple silver design, earlier versions were of a more heraldic style in shape with a blue background.

Dacia cars were named after the historical name of the region where their factory is located at Mioveni, near Piteşti in modern-day Romania.

The Dacia company was initially entitled Uzina de Autoturisme Piteşti (meaning Pitesti car factory) and orignally produced licensed versions of Renault cars for the local market. Renault would eventually take them over as a subsiduary in 1999.

The Dacia shield is a design of classic simplicity. Early versions had the name on a blue shield while later versions such as this are far simpler.

DAF

Produced: 1958–1976.

The Badge: The DAF badge depicts a gear wheel with a leaf suspension spring behind. The company name is written in bold letters above the wheel while the location of the factory is written above and below the centre of the wheel (Eidhoven across the top, Nederland around the lower rim).

The initials 'DAF' stand for Van Doorne's Automobiel Fabriek (Doorne's Automobile Factory) after the name of the company's managing director. Previously it had been known as Doorne's Aanhangwagen Fabriek (Doorne's Trailer Factory), also abbreviated to DAF.

DAF effectively only made one vehicle, despite there being a range of model-specific designations. In the UK all were effectively known as Variomatic after their innovative transmission system. Many years ahead of the time, it substituted moving belts in place of fixed-gear gearbox ratios to offer a continuously variable gear ratio to suit the driving conditions.

Volvo took an interest in the company and late model variomatics were badged as Volvos. What would become the Volvo 340 would have been a DAF model had Volvo not purchased the company.

The DAF badge highlights the gearwheel of the unique Variomatic gearing system for which they were famous.

Now known as the Nedcar factory, today the old DAF factory produces Smart cars and Minis, while previously it has produced Mitsubishi Colt hatchbacks for the European market.

Daihatsu

Produced: 1907–date.

The Badge: Daihatsu cars wear an elongated and stylised 'D' of the initial letter of their name surrounded by a chrome oval. When the Campagno saloon came to the UK it wore a fictional heraldic shield on the grille, but this was never used again.

Daihatsu's parent company was formed in 1907 as the Hatsudoki Seizo Company with the aim of manufacturing internal combustion engines for other manufacturers to use. The company name changed in 1951 to Daihatsu, a combination of the Japanese words for Osaka (the character for the 'O' in Osaka can also be pronounced 'Dai') where they were based, and the term 'engine manufacturer'.

In 1965, Daihatsu was the first Japanese marque imported to England in the form of the Campagno (meaning 'companion') saloon, and became the first Japanese car to be tested by *Autocar* magazine.

The bold italic 'D' of the Daihatsu badge is in stark contrast to the faux heraldic badge design of their first offering on the UK market.

Daimler

Produced: 1896–2007.

The Badge: Daimlers are badged with a simple Daimler script with a large flourish from the initial 'D' arching over the full length of the word. During the 1950s the legend 'England' was added below the word 'Daimler'.

Almost all models wore a variation of the distinctive fluted grille, surmounted by an ornate 'D' insignia as seen at the start of the full Daimler name badge.

British Daimler have been manufacturing cars since the dawn of motoring, competing in the first motorcar journey from Land's End to John O'Groats in 1897. Originally the British arm of German company Daimler-Benz, they would go on to hold the royal warrant for many years, also becoming known for their commercial vehicles.

Letters followed by number were the way Daimlers were designated for many years. The 'D' stood for Daimler and the second letter was used in order over the years, although some did have specific meanings. Their DH (Daimler Hire) range would become well known for their limousines.

Later models would use names taken from royalty such as the Regency, Empress and Regina. Their first (relatively) small saloon would be christened Conquest as the price before tax was £1,066, the date of the Norman invasion of England.

When purchased by Jaguar, Daimler models became more luxurious versions of Jaguars, retaining their famous fluted grille.

The front of the Daimler SP250 shows the neat Daimler script nose badge as well as a version of the famous fluted grille. The presence of the Turner designed V8 under the bonnet is quietly indicated by the chrome 'V' designed into the grille.

Datsun

Produced: 1911–86, 2012–date.

The Badge: The full Datsun badge, in full colour, is the company name in a blue rectangle over the Rising Sun flag of Japan. Later rendered in chrome as a grille badge, it was described as representing modernisation and sophistication. Eventually the Datsun name was replaced by Nissan when the Datsun named was dropped in 1986.

DAT, the company that would eventually become Datsun, was founded in 1911 by Sotaro Hasimoto and was named after the initials of the surnames of investors Denjiro Den, Rokuro Aoyama and Meitaro Takuchi.

First producing trucks, in 1931 the Son of DAT, their first car, was launched as Datson. As Son in Japanese translates as 'great loss', it was changed to Datsun, and a marque was born. The 'sun' of the word Datsun is also considered a tribute to the Japanese Rising Sun flag.

Industrial company Nissan took over Datsun in 1934 and in time their name would replace that of Datsun across the centre of the badge. The legend 'Datsun – Product of Nissan' was regularly seen in their brochures.

The Datsun name was resurrected by Nissan in 2012 as a brand of value-for-money vehicles in specific markets.

The full colour version of the Datsun badge as shown in one of their catalogues. Even in this early 1970s version the Nissan name is prominently displayed as the parent company. Reproduced with permission of Nissan UK.

By the late 1980s the Nissan name had replaced that of Datsun across the centre bar of the badge.

De Tomaso

Produced: 1963–date.

The Badge: The De Tomaso badge is derived from the founder's initials, usually displayed over a vertical rendition of his native Argentinian flag.

Alejando de Tomaso was born in Argentina in 1928, the son of a former prime minister. Political pressures forced him to flee Argentina in 1955 and he moved to Italy. There he

The Argentinian flag makes a bold background to the De Tomaso badge and pays homage to the founder's country of birth.

married the wealthy American Elizabeth Haskell and formed the car company that would come to bear his name. Fully, De Tomaso Automobili spA.

His first car was launched in 1963 in the form of the Vallelunga (named after a famous racing circuit), followed by the Mangusta ('mongoose' in Italian, a dig at the AC/Shelby Cobras he was racing). Later would come the Pantera (panther) and touring car the Longchamps (long legs)

In quick succession De Tomaso would have control of Maserati (he would sell them to FIAT), Moto Guzzi motorcycles and Innocenti, builders of unique Minis for the Italian market.

DeLorean

Produced: 1981–83.
The Badge: DeLorean cars (there was only one model) wore a horizontal black grille bearing the letters 'DMC' in a stylised sans-serif font, the 'D' missing the left hand upright of the letter. The letters stood for the initials of the company, the DeLorean Motor Company.

John DeLorean produced the car that bore his name in a factory in Northern Ireland, part financed by the government to bring employment to what was an area of high unemployment. The vehicle was assembled from propriety mechanical parts housed in a unique body as many small-scale manufacturers had done before him.

The bold DMC badge of the De Lorean motor company was both modern and simple in execution, the DMC standing for De Lorean Motor Company.

Plagued by poor reviews and build quality, quickly followed by the arrest (and subsequent acquittal) of John DeLorean himself, the company quickly folded. It remains most famous for the part it played in the film *Back to the Future* and its signature gullwing doors.

EMW

Produced: 1945–55.

The Badge: As the EMW factory was effectively building BMW clones, they used the established BMW roundel badge but coloured the usual blue segments in Communist red and added the title of the company around the edge of the badge.

After the Second World War the BMW factory at Eisenach found itself in the Russian-occupied area of post-war Germany. Under Russian control production of the BMW models was restarted, but rather than the old BMW title, they were marketed as EMWs, standing for Eisenach Motor Works (Eisenacher MotorenWerke in full, meaning Eisenach motor factory).

Production at the factory would continue for many years after the EMW badge was abandoned in 1955, the factory turning to building Wartburgs among others.

The red and white EMW roundel was directly descended from the BMW roundel which had previously produced at the Eisenacher factory.

Ferrari

Produced: 1947–date.

The Badge: During his racing driving career Enzo Ferrari, after whom the company was named, won races at the Savio Circuit. He found himself being awarded his prizes by, and came to know well, Count Baracca, son of First World War fighter pilot Ace Franceso Baracca.

When Ferrari started to manufacture cars under his own name Francesco's widow, Countess Paolina Baracca, gave him permission (some say she persuaded him) to use Baracca's personal prancing horse emblem on his cars. Ferrari set the prancing horse on a yellow shield as yellow was considered the colour of Modena where he was based.

Ferrari would add the colours of the Italian flag to the top of the badge in honour of his home country and where the cars were manufactured. The letters 'SF' on the bottom of the badge mean Scuderia (team) Ferrari.

Many Ferraris bore numbers rather than model names, but his son Dino was immortalised as the name of a small model built and badged as a FIAT, but now better known as the Ferrari Dino.

As fashions changed later Ferraris had names. The Daytona was named to honour his cars' successes at the American 24-hour race of the same name. The famous Testa Rossa (once voted the most popular poster car in the world) translates literally as 'Red Head' after the colour the engine cylinder heads were painted, and this was in turn a homage to the engine of an earlier racing Ferrari.

The Ferrari prancing horse remains one of the best-known images in motoring. Rumour has it the company makes more from their merchandising of it than they do from car sales.

FIAT

Produced: 1899–date.

The Badge: Over the years there have been a number of developments of the FIAT badge. Early models wore a simple script badge, which was replaced by the bold FIAT legend on a circular enamel boss surrounded by a winner's garland to signify their racing successes.

For a time in the 1980s, while smooth aerodynamic bonnets were the fashion and radiator grilles not openly present, FIAT badged the front of their cars with a small chrome representation of a FIAT grille.

The FIAT name stands for Fabbrica Italiana Automobili Torino, which translates into English as 'Italian automobile manufacturers of Turin'.

FIAT's most famous offering, the 500, was named after the engine capacity of the car. Their much later small model called Cinquecento translates as the same in Italian, and the Seicento that followed it being 600 in Italian, a homage to the earlier following model.

Other well-known models included the Strada (street), Uno (number one) and Multipa (Multiple, as befitting an early people carrier.).

Most other FIAT models had numbers rather than names, although for a time FIAT manufactured a range of large cars under the SuperFiat brand name.

The FIAT roundel in a range of forms was the badge of most FIATs for many years.

During the 1980s, while radiator grilles were not visible for styling reasons FIAT adopted this tiny representation of their grille as a bonnet badge on their cars.

Ford

Produced: 1911–date (UK).

The Badge: Ford cars are badged with a simple oval script badge of the word 'Ford'. It was once thought to be a copy of the company founder's signature, but Ford now deny this, saying it was designed by a friend and graphic designer using a suitably artistic font.

Initially stamped into the bronze of early radiator surrounds, it was standardised displayed within an oval blue field. During the 1980s a colour-coded field behind the word that matched the car paintwork was a marker that the car was a press vehicle.

In common with many of their competitors, during the 1950s Ford UK cars would occasionally wear a faux heraldic device on their grilles, theirs with the legend 'made in England' beneath.

Henry Ford founded the Henry Ford Company in 1901, but soon left (it would go on to become Cadillac) and set up the Ford Motor Company in 1903.

The early models would be described with a letter, the letters being used in order – A, etc. – the most famous of which would be the long-lived Model T, which would remain in production until 1927.

Their UK family of small cars was the Anglia, Popular and Prefect, models that would be regularly updated. Anglia had two doors, while Prefect had four. The Popular name would be resurrected many years later as a trim level denoting a value for money model. Estate cars would be given the country-gentry-inspired name Squire and described with the old-fashioned term 'Shooting brake'.

Much later there were models named after exotic holiday destinations such as Cortina, Capri and Granada.

The Ford badge is probably the widest distributed car badge in the world. Initially the signature was stamped in the brass of early Ford radiators, but it soon became a separate badge across all their ranges.

The simple, bold FSO badge devoid of decoration was indicative of the car's utilitarian origins.

FSO

Produced: 1978–2002.
The Badge: FSO cars wore a simple silver/chrome rendition of the marque name in a bold, sans-serif font.

FSO stood for the initial letters of the company name, Fabryka Samochodów Osobowych, which translates from Polish as 'Passenger Car Factory'.

Their only product was a hatchback based on the licence-produced Polski-FIAT 125, replacing the old square FIAT body with a more modern hatchback style. It was named Polonez after the traditional Polish dance the Polonaise. The name was chosen through a poll conducted in the Polish newspaper *Życie Warszawy* to select a name for the new car.

Ghia

Produced/In Use: 1916–date.
The Badge: Early Ghia vehicles were badged with large chrome version of the signature of the company founder, Giacinto Ghia. When he died in 1944 the rights to his name and goodwill were purchased by designers Mario Boano and Giorgio Alberti. They created the shield-style badge we know today.

The signature of Giacinto Ghia was faithfully reproduced along a blue stripe that ran upwards across the red heraldic shield with a crown above.

Initially a coachbulding company, Ghia came under the control of De Tomaso cars, and as part of a deal to get his Ford-powered cars into Ford showrooms in the USA he sold them the rights to use the Ghia name. Ford used the Ghia name as a mark of the top level of trim on many of their model ranges until 2010. A small Ghia badge was usually fitted just ahead of the 'A' post on the front wing to denote this luxurious trim level.

The Ghia shield was a development of the original signature badge seen on such cars as the Karmann Ghia. Today it is better remembered as a trim level on luxury Fords, the long coachbuilding history forgotten.

Gilbern

Produced: 1959–73.

The Badge: As befitting the only car manufactured in Wales, Gilbern adopted the Welsh dragon as their badge.

Gilbern was formed by the unlikely duo of Welsh master butcher Giles Smith and German ex-POW Bernard Frieze, a fibreglass engineer. By amalgamating the first parts of their Christian names, the 'GIL' of Giles and the 'BERN' of Bernard, the Gilbern motorcar was born.

Initially a sporty fibreglass coupe that started life as a personal project, production would move from the slaughterhouse behind the Giles Smith butchers shop to a small factory constructed on a nearby redundant colliery site when orders started to arrive.

The Gilbern Welsh Dragon badge was inspired by the location of their factory near Pontypridd in South Wales.

Healey

See Austin Healey.

Hillman

Produced: 1907–78.

The Badge: Hillman cars were badged with a winged device in bold letters of the company name with the famous three church spires of Coventry (the Old Cathedral Church of St Michael, Holy Trinity and Christ Church), where the company was based, visible in the background.

Much later models produced under the Rootes Group had far simpler badges, with three chrome spikes to represent the spires on a plain background.

Initially known as Hillman-Coatelen after the two founders William Hillman and Louis Coatalen, when Coatalen moved on in 1910 the company became simply known as Hillman Motors.

The year 1932 saw the launch of the Hillman Minx, a name that would remain with Hillman for many years. Designed as basic, quality transport, it was joined by a sporting version called the Aero Minx (flying Minx) and later restyled into the Minx Magnificient. There was also a series of large, luxury models known as the Hillman Wizard.

After the Second World War there would be an American-inspired model named Californian after the state. Models with two-tone paint would be titled 'Gay look' after the use of the word at the time as signifying being fun. The standard fitment of a radio would see a version christened the Melody Minx. A larger Hillman called the Hunter would be named after the company chairman.

The small Imp (a small evil spirit) was built at a new government-sponsored factory at Linwood in Scotland. An advanced design, it would sadly live up to the name.

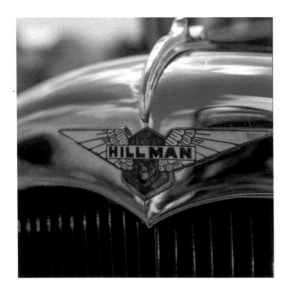

The original Hillman badge depicted the skyline of Coventry in great detail. Later badges under the Rootes group were less impressive, reducing the three Spires to three simple chrome points on a solid-coloured field.

The last completely fresh design from Hillman was the martially named Avenger in 1969, which would remarkably be produced under three badges until production ceased in 1981. In 1977, it would be rebadged Chrysler after Hillman's new owners, and briefly Talbot before production ceased.

The last incarnation of the Hunter name found fame when the GT version (note: it was a Hillman GT, never Hunter GT) won the London–Sydney rally in 1968.

Long after its European demise, the Hillman Hunter was still being assembled from British-sourced kits in Iran as the Peykan (Arrow, after the company designation of the last Hunter-badged cars, the 'Arrow' range). Iranian production continued until 2005, eventually with newer Avenger-derived engines and an interior from the Talbot Alpine. The production tools were then sold on to a company in Sudan, so the Hunter may someday rise again.

The Hillman/Rootes Group commercial range was badged Commer, a simple shortening of the term Commercial.

Honda

Produced: 1963–date.

The Badge: The company badge is a simple chrome 'H' within a bounding chrome surround.

Soichiro Honda, the company founder and man who would give his name to the company, was born in 1906 in Iwatagun in Japan.

After the Second World War Honda founded the Honda Technical Research Laboratory. His first product involved the fitting of small army surplus generators to bicycle frames to create a cheap, basic form of transport.

The first Honda motorcycle arrived in 1949, and was called the Dream because Honda had a dream of speed. The company would soon become the largest motorcycle producer in the world. Their first production four-wheeler was a van in 1963.

Honda retired as company president in 1974, taking instead the title of supreme advisor, still guiding the moves and policies of his company. He passed away in August 1991.

The simple elegance of the Honda badge requires no introduction to motorists anywhere. It was inspired by the initial letter of the surname of the company founder.

Hudson

Produced: 1909–57.

The Badge: Hudson cars wear the Hudson company crest, or the company name in bold blue with a gold edging over the company address on a white triangular field.

The crest had twin turrets, which signified the ruggedness of the design, and twin ships, which represented the adventure the car could bring into the buyer's life. The ships were inspired by the designs of the ships that had brought the original members of the Hudson family to America.

Joseph Hudson financed the Hudson Motor Car Company in 1909. He was the wealthy owner of a department store in Detroit and gave financial backing to engineer Howard Earle Coffin and salesman Roy Dikeman Chapin to start the Hudson Car Company. They would lead to Hudson becoming the third-largest car producer in the USA by the late 1920s, behind Ford and Chevrolet.

Famous for retaining their straight eight engine long after others had moved on to the quintessential American V8, their range of smaller vehicles were called Essex (a name acquired when Hudson brought that company), Terraplane (a name without a specific meaning, but which would be reused for a series of French hovercraft) and Pacemaker (a racing reference) would follow.

The Hudson car was financed by the owner of the huge Hudson shop chain, based in Detroit. Once established they would wear a crest inspired by the ships that the brought the Hudson family to America.

Humber

Produced: 1899–1976.

The Badge: Early Humbers wore a simple Humber script badge, while later models had the name spelt out across the bonnet in separate chrome letters.

The company was named after its founder, Thomas Humber. In the early days there were two Humber factories: one at Beeston in Nottinghamshire where the luxury models were produced, and one in Coventry where they manufactured their mass-produced vehicles.

After the First World War, Humber bought Hillman cars and Commer vans, while in 1929 Humber was in turn taken over by the Rootes Group.

Perhaps the most famous Humber was General Bernard Law Montgomery's wartime staff car, immortalised for generations of schoolboys by the Airfix kit.

Humber cars were often aimed at the Rolls-Royce market and often wore such grand names as Pullman (named after a luxury train carriage) and Imperial (relating to an empire). Lesser models were named after birds such as Hawk and Snipe, while a better specified model would become the Super Snipe.

In the face of falling sale in the 1960s, Rootes created the Humber Sceptre (named after a heraldic staff), a luxury family saloon based on a Hillman body. It ran through two versions before the Humber name was discontinued in 1976.

In later years the Humber name was displayed as single chrome letters across the nose of their vehicles.

The apparently simple 'H' of the Hyundai badge hides a hidden meaning of satisfaction between company representative and the purchaser of a Hyundai car.

Hyundai

Produced: 1968–date.

The Badge: Hyundai cars are badged with a simple italic silver 'H'. One side of the 'H' represents the company representative and the other a satisfied customer leaning towards each other and shaking hands.

Hyundai (which means 'modern') is South Korea's largest industrial company with interests in many fields. From 1968 they assembled British Ford cars and from 1974 they produced vehicles of their own design.

Masterminded by British George Turnbull, previously employed by both Standard-Triumph and the Austin-Morris division of British Leyland, he organised a simple design styled by Giugiaro with running gear by Mitsubishi, christened Pony.

In 1974, it was launched as basic, reliable transport. Current models have numbers rather than names – the larger the number, the larger the vehicle. The 4 x 4 market is served by the Santa Fe, named after the American town to bring the romance of the American prairies to the range and no doubt remind people of the iconic Jeep brand.

Jaguar

Produced: 1945–date.

The Badge: Jaguars have all worn a variation of the Jaguar 'Big Cat' badge. Early models had bonnet mascots of the leaping cat until safety legislation forced later models to make do with a flat badge of the Jaguar's head viewed from the front (known as 'The Growler') on their bonnet. When the bonnet mascot was reintroduced, it became known as 'The Leaper'.

Entrepreneur William Lyons founded what was to become Jaguar Cars when he signed his first factory lease on his twenty-first birthday in 1922. His early models were badged SS (see their own entry), and after the Second World War the whole range adopted the name Jaguar, previously only used on the most sporting models.

The Jaguar Leaper and Growler shown together on the front of a Jaguar. Most models would have one or other, but a lucky few had both.

The post-Second World War saloons carried on the mark numbering from the pre-war cars, skipping the Mk VI as Bentley had only recently used this designation. This would continue until the vast Mk X (all models used Roman numerals), after which the separate large saloon range was discontinued.

The sports car range would be given a model name prefixed by XK, after the company designation for their twin-cam engine. This was suffixed by a number that was a reflection of the vehicles top speed (e.g. the XK120 was powered by the XK engine and was capable of 120 miles per hour).

The Racing Jaguars at Le Mans became known as 'Competition' or 'C' types, and as they progressed they sequentially became the 'D' type and eventually the famous roadgoing 'E' type. As a nod to the pre-war cars, there was very briefly an XKSS road car based on the racing 'D' type.

Late model XK150 sports models would proudly wear a red and orange circular badge on their boot lids listing Jaguars' numerous successes at the Le Mans 24-hour race.

JCB

Produced: 1945–date.
The Badge: JCB vehicles are badged in a distinctive sans-serif font, with the letters growing smaller right to left and surrounded in an elongated outline. Traditionally, all JCB machines are presented in a bright yellow livery that many other manufacturers have also embraced.

The geometric JCB badge is often ignored hidden discretely away on their bright yellow earth movers, but it represents one of the UK's success stories.

The JCB company was formed in 1945 by Joseph Cyril Bamford, who gave his initials to the venture. The JCB logo as we know it today arrived in 1953, emblazoned on the side of the yellow machines known worldwide as the 'JCB', technically termed a back hoe excavator. The term JCB even entered the Oxford English dictionary as meaning 'earth moving equipment'.

The JCB found fame with their 3C model, which is best recalled by those that used it for the then unique inclusion of facilities in the operator's cab for boiling a kettle.

Jeep

Produced: 1941–date.
The Badge: The signature of the Jeep is the styling feature of a number of vertical radiator grille gaps rather than a badge. These were first seen on the pressed steel cheap and easy to assemble wartime jeep and have been carried forward to modern examples. Originally there were nine; on modern Jeeps this has been reduced to seven. Now less functional, they make the front of every Jeep instantly recognisable.

The embryo vertical grille slats that now identify all Jeep models are clearly seen on this wartime model.

There are two theories regarding the origins of the Jeep name. The most likely is that when the US army commissioned a new general-purpose vehicle it was officially known by the initial letters 'GP'. This became roughly pronounced as 'Jeep'. The other theory is that it was somehow nicknamed after a Popeye character called Eugene the Jeep, and the name stuck.

Jeep doesn't have a make in its own right. Much like the Mini, it has always been known as the Jeep, whatever manufacturer's badge it was wearing at the time. Currently the Jeep brand is owned by FIAT-Chrysler.

Once in civilian life most Jeep models were given names based on cowboy archetypes such as Wrangler, Renegade, etc. The CJ (or civilian jeep) series ran for many years through a range of numbered variants.

Jensen

Produced: 1935–76.

The Badge: Jensen cars wear a triple-level winged badge with the wings widest at the top and growing narrower towards the base. The word 'Jensen' is written across a red central section with flourishes above and/or below depending on the era. On later models the wings would be reduced to a much more restrained style in keeping with fashion.

Jensen Healeys would substitute a modern graphic design of a bold 'H' with the words 'Jensen' above the centre bar and 'Healey' below.

Company founders, brothers Allan and Richard Jensen, after whom the company was named, christened their first car simply the Jensen Convertible. Powered by an American V8, a specially modified example was purchased by Hollywood star Clark Gable, a replica of which was marketed as the 'Gable replica'.

The Interceptor family of 1966 saw the world's first production 4 x 4 road car: the FF. The FF stood for Formula Ferguson, the name of the variable four-wheel-drive system

Above left: Both the angular original and later squared-off badges are visible on this Jensen FF, famous for bringing permanent four-wheel drive to the sports coupe market.

Above right: When Donald Healey joined forces with Jensen the new badge that emerged was bold and simple in keeping with the fashion of the times.

being utilised. It was also the first production car to feature anti-lock brakes as standard in the form of the Dunlop Maxaret system.

Donald Healey of Austin Healey fame joined the company, and both designed and gave his name to the Jensen Healey sports car, designed around a Lotus engine and Vauxhall running gear.

Jowett

Produced: 1906–54.
The Badge: The Jowett badge consisted of the Jowett name in script, often over an image of their signature flat twin engine in profile.

The company was named after founders William and Benjamin Jowett. They developed a tough flat twin-cylindered engine that would remain in production from 1906 until 1953. It is best remembered for powering the Bradford van (named after the town in which the company was based).

In 1947, Jowett surprised the world by the introduction the advanced Jowett Javelin (meaning fast moving and streamlined) saloon, powered by a four-cylinder development of their twin-cylinder engine. Even more briefly, from 1950 to 1954, was a sports car based on the Javelin called the Jupiter, named after the planet.

Most famous for fronting the Bradford van, the Jowett name would end its days on the sporting Javelin and Jupiter cars.

The KIA badge is an exercise in bold modern design. Very early versions would depict the letters as factory chimneys complete with artistic smoke.

KIA

Produced: 1944–date (as a company), 1952–date (vehicles).

The Badge: The KIA badge is a simple rendition of the company initials. Very early models depicted the initials as the chimneys of a factory complete with smoke, but this soon gave way to the simpler rendition.

The KIA company name is made up of two Sino-Korean characters 'Ki' ('to arise') and 'A' ('the east'), effectively translating the company name as 'Rising from the East'.

Kia model names have included Pride (of ownership) and Santa Fe, which was named to appeal to the initial American market.

Lada

Produced: 1970–date.

The Badge: The badge of a sailing ship was chosen for Lada cars as they were in common use by the local river pirates (some describe them as Vikings) for which the area where the factory was built was once well known. These boats were colloquially known as 'Ladya', which was adapted as a name for the new Russian car marque to be built at the AutoVaz factory.

Lada ('beloved one' in Russian) cars are manufactured in the city of Togliattigrad in west Russia. The original iconic Lada saloon is better known locally as 'Zhiguli' after the hills surrounding the factory, the name often being altered for export to allow easier pronunciation in non-Russian-speaking markets. In local slang it was also known as 'Kopeyka' after the small denomination coin, and under the Soviet system it was officially known as Small Class, Passenger Car Model One.

With assistance from FIAT production began of a modified version of the FIAT 124 (known at FIAT as the 124R, R for Russian) saloon with a simplified engine for easier maintenance in rural Russia. There was even briefly a high performance Wankel rotary-engined version available only to the police.

Seen here as depicted in an early sales brochure, the 'Ladya' after which the car was named refers to boat depicted on the badge. Picture reproduced with permission of Lada cars.

The more advanced hatchback Samara (named after a town near the factory) followed the saloon in 1984, while the tiny but incredibly capable Niva (meaning 'cornfield') four-wheel drive was popular all around the world.

Lagonda

Produced: 1906–date (with gaps).

The Badge: An extravagant, winged rendition of the marque name is worn above the grille of most Lagonda models. Early examples were brass with a blue enamel inlay while later ones were rendered in chrome with a red enamel inlay. When David Brown of Aston Martin fame purchased the company he added his name above that of Lagonda.

The Lagonda badge was a particularly extravagant variation on the traditional winged name badge style. Versions used while controlled by David Brown owned Aston Martin put his name above the Lagonda name on the badge.

The company was started in the UK by American Wilbur Gunn, former opera singer and keen engineer. He named his company after the Shawnee Indian name for his home town of Buck Creek in Springfield, Ohio. His brother had already used the name for his own company, the Lagonda Corporation, which made cleaning machinery.

In common with many marques, early models were listed by engine sizes and power outputs. When Lagonda was taken over by Aston Martin it would become a model name i.e. The Aston Martin Lagonda. It was usually an upmarket four-door model closely derived from the sportier Aston Martin models.

Lamborghini

Produced: 1947–date.

The Badge: There are two popularly repeated explanations for the adoption of the Raging Bull badge on Lamborghinis. One suggests that it was chosen as the company founder was a Taurean; the other is that he was fan of bull fighting.

Ferriccio Lamborghini, company founder and who gave the company its name, was a trained engineer who began tuning FIATs during the 1930s.

The first vehicles to wear the now famous Raging Bull badge were tractors. Following an argument with Ferrari over build quality he decided to start building high-performance cars of his own.

Most Lamborghinis are named after bulls, bull breeds or items relating to bull fighting. Famous models included the Muira (named after a particularly wild breed of fighting bull), Islero (named after a bull who killed a famous matador), Espada (a sword), Urraco (a slang term meaning 'Little Bull'), Jalpa (another breed of fighting bull), Gallardo (a further bull breed), Aventador (a prize-winning bull breed) and Huracan (a specific, famous bull from 1879).

The most famous Lamborghini was the Countach. This word is considered a not entirely polite term used by Piedmontese natives as a sign of amazement. There was also a Lamborghini Diablo, which quite literally translates to 'Devil'.

Lanchester

Produced: 1900–55.

The Badge: Lanchester cars wore their marque name written in a serif typeface, usually with the heights peaking in the centre of the word.

The Lanchester company was formed by the Lanchester brothers Frederick, George and Frank. Frederick would come to be one of the most influential automotive engineers of his era and their designs were advanced for their time. It is claimed that Lanchester produced the first British motorcar design in 1895, and some claim it was the first in the world.

Nearly always badged with engine outputs rather than names, the Lanchester marque itself passed to BSA, then following their purchase to Daimler. Daimler was later purchased by Jaguar, and the name now resides with Jaguar Land Rover, still listed as an active company.

Lancia

Produced: 1907–date.

The Badge: Lancia translates from Italian to 'lance', and the badges used on Lancias all feature a derivation of the word. Some show the name impaled on a lance, more commonly on a flag flying from an upright lance. More recently it is displayed as a flag/lance insignia over an image of a four-spoke steering wheel on a blue shield.

The company was founded by Vincenzo Lancia and he would give his name to the cars. Although far from being his first car, Lancia's first famous car was the Lambda, named after the eleventh letter of the Greek alphabet and wearing that letter as a badge. Later the Greek alphabet would also name the Beta (the second letter of their alphabet), Gamma (the third letter), Delta (the fourth) Epsilon (the fifth) and Kappa (the ninth). Other model names used would include the Aurelia (meaning 'golden'), Aprilia ('youthful'), Flavia ('golden blonde'), Fulvia ('blonde one'), Stratos ('army') and Monte Carlo (named after the rally).

For a time, most Lancias were available as a performance version under the HF banner (standing for High Fidelity) and wearing an elephant badge. This badge was a tribute to early Lancia wins in the Alpine Rally and a homage to General Hannibal, who in ancient times crossed the Alps with elephants to support his army in battle.

Above: The HF, or high fidelity high performance, Lancias wore elephants in homage to Hannibal after his crossing of the Alps with elephants. The initial HF models had been successful in the Alpine rally so they adopted his elephants as their symbol.

Left: The full Lancia badge of the flag on the lance displayed over a steering wheel. Over the year there have been many variations of the flag on the lance theme.

The intricate Lea Francis badge features a Burmese temple figure after one of the company founders travelled to the country and sketched it.

Lea Francis

Produced: 1903–1960.

The Badge: The Lea Francis badge shows a depiction of a Burmese unicorn. The Burmese temple figure shows a fish's tail with a unicorn's head, while others refers to is as a Burmese version of the mythical Hippocampus. Before it are the initials of the company name, L and F, with the creature's hooves resting upon them. The Burmese figure was sketched by one of the company founders during a tour of Burma and adopted as their badge, presumably to bring them luck.

Richard Henry Lea and Graham Inglesby Francis founded what would become Lea Francis cars in 1895. Initially known for their top-quality bicycles, car production began in 1903. They formed a partnership with Vulcan cars, under which Vulcan supplied Lea Francis with bodies in return for having their running gear manufactured by Lea Francis.

Lea Francis were most famous for their Hyper model (meaning 'energetic'), claimed to be the world's first production supercharged vehicle, and later the Acre of Spades, named after what is regarded as the highest scoring playing card in the deck.

Their last vehicle was the famously purple with gold chrome Lynx (named after the jungle cat) displayed at the 1960 motor show.

Lotus

Produced: 1952–date.

The Badge: The Lotus badge was designed to resemble the Lotus flower in the colours yellow and green. The green section was a tribute to the traditional British racing green colour used on British racing cars, and the yellow colour signified what company founder Chapman hoped were the sunlit times ahead for his company.

Above left: The original colourful Lotus badge surmounted by the company founder's initials. After 1968 it was rendered in silver over black after the death of racing driver Jim Clark.

Above right: From 1982 Lotus cars wore this simpler black badge, still surmounted by the founder's initials, to mark his passing

The word 'Lotus' was written around the lower edge of the green segment of the badge in a simple font, while Chapman placed a combination design of his full set of initials above the lettering.

Following the death of world champion racing driver Jim Clark in 1968, the badge was changed to a silver on black design as a mark of respect. Then from 1982 Lotus models would just be badged with the famous Chapman initials in gold over the word 'Lotus' on a black badge in honour of the company founder's passing.

When company founder Anthony Colin Bruce Chapman (hence the set of four superimposed initials on the badge) created his first car, it is rumoured to have been named after a term of endearment he used towards his girlfriend, whom he referred to as his 'lotus blossom'.

Others say he chose the word lotus as the lotus fruit, when consumed, created a state of bliss as he hoped would be felt by the owners of his cars during their ownership. The exact truth will always be a matter of speculation as, in the words of the company, 'the truth died with Chapman'.

During the 1960s Lotus found fame in television as a supplier for cars for the heroes of ITC television shows. The Prisoner drove a Lotus seven and both Emma Peel and Tara King of the *Avengers* would drive their products.

For 1973 the Esprit (meaning a lively spirit) could wear a badge on the rear detailing the long list of Lotus racing cars Formula One championship wins from 1963 to 1973.

Build quality issues would lead some unkind mechanics to say that Lotus actually stood for 'Loads of trouble usually serious'.

Marcos

Produced: 1959–2007.

The Badge: The Marcos badge is the company name set in a blue oval within a geometric shape with points top and bottom and a red stripe running upwards left to right. The exact origin of the symbol has been lost in the mists of time, and the badges themselves are for some reason infamously fragile.

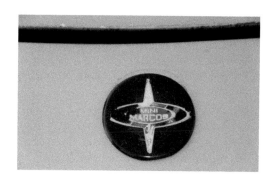

The origins of the geometric and famously fragile Marcos badge are lost in the mists of time. This example badges the tiny Mini Marcos, which took both engine and suspension subframes from the Mini car.

The company was famous for making their cars with a wooden monocoque inspired by the De Haviland Mosquito and Vampire wood-based warplanes produced where the company founders had worked. It was founded by Jem Marsh and Frank Costin. They would each take the first three letters of each of their surnames to create the company name: MARsh and COStin.

Maserati

Produced: 1926–date.

The Badge: The Maserati Trident badge was inspired by the statue of Neptune at the large fountain in the Piazza Maggiore in Bologna where the company was founded. Officially a blue trident set in a white oval with blue waves beneath, it is more frequently seen rendered as a simple chrome design.

Maserati cars was founded by Maserati brothers Alfieri, Bindo, Carlo, Ettore, and Ernesto.

Model names would include Quattroporte (literally 'four doors'), Ghibli (named after an Egyptian wind), Mistral (a winter wind), Khamsin (an Egyptian wind that blows in the spring) Bora ('let's go'), Merak ('wonder') and Kyalami (named after an African motor racing circuit).

The long-lived and relatively cheap Bi-Turbo range was an attempt to increase sales and was named after the engine's most famous feature; that it had two turbos attached to the V6 engine.

Not a badge, but a famous design feature seen on all Maserati cars, is an oval analogue clock on the middle of the dashboard.

The Maserati Trident has been used a range of variations over the years, the simple chrome version being the most common.

The Mclaren badge denotes some of the fastest road cars ever produced yet is plain and simple in execution. The red 'tick' represents the swirling air behind a fast-moving car.

Mclaren

Produced: 1992, then 2011–date.
The Badge: Production Mclaren road cars are badged with a simple chrome on black logo of the company name with an artistic red tick above the 'N'. The tick is said to represent the air vortices created behind a car when travelling at speed.

Based in England, Mclaren have been manufacturing racing cars since 1965. They were founded by New Zealand born mechanic Bruce Mclaren from whose name the company takes its name

They achieved a remarkable number of driver and constructor championships before turning their skills to road cars. They produced a limited edition vehicle called the F1 (in honour of their Formula One successes) in 1992, not returning to road vehicles until 2011.

Mercedes Benz

Produced: 1901–date.
The Badge: The Mercedes Benz badge is a chrome three-pointed star within a circle. When laid flat as a bonnet badge it has a surrounding winners garland to celebrate their successes in motorsport. The legend 'Mercedes' is written across the top of the circle and 'Benz' around the bottom.

As is frequently the case, there are conflicting stories of how Mercedes came by their badge. The official version is that the three-pointed star was derived from the three types of machines powered by their engines: motor cars, ships and aeroplanes. Currently the company describes it as symbolising their domination of land, sea and air. Earlier versions have it that the three-pointed star was derived from a lucky symbol used by Gottleib Daimler.

The full Mercedes badge and bonnet mascot are seldom seen together like this. According to Mercedes, there is one point of the star for each of the markets they serve: land, sea and air.

Gottlieb Daimler (whose name would be retained by the British branch of the company) set up an engineering company with Wilhelm Maybach (whose name would later grace top of the range Mercedes cars) in 1882. Daimler died in 1899 and his place was taken on the board by car enthusiast Emil Jellinek. Jellinek had a daughter named Mercedes (Spanish for 'Grace'), and her name was adopted for all Daimlers supplied to the French market for legal licensing reasons. All German-built Daimlers also came to be badged 'Mercedes' from 1902.

The 'Benz' part of the name arrived in 1926 when they merged with a rival motoring company formed by Karl Benz.

Mercedes cars are currently badged by a letter indicating where the model sits in the range. The further the letter is along in the alphabet the larger the car, i.e. the A class is smaller than the C class. The following number indicates the engine size.

Messerschmitt

Produced: 1953–61.
The Badge: The Messerschmitt initially shared the insignia (an upright depiction of a bird) of the aeroplane manufacturer that built the car while not allowed by treaty to build military aeroplanes. Later models wore a horizontal line of three upright squares containing the letters 'FMR'. These stood for Fahrzeug-und Maschinenbau Regensberg (Vehicle and Mechanical Engineering, Regensberg). Regensberg was the town in Bavaria where they were manufactured. The company that took over the production of the car after Messerschmitt were permitted to restart aeroplane production.

A rare four-wheeled Messerschmitt clearly displays the more common three box style of badge. Early versions were badged with Messerschmitt's upright bird insignia.

The Messerschmitt micro-car was known as the Kabinenroller (literally 'Cabin Scooter', colloquially known in Spanish-speaking markets as the 'German Mouse'). It was the production version of a vehicle for disabled ex-servicemen designed by aircraft designer Fritz Fend. Originally called the Flitzer, it was initially powered by an engine originally designed as the starter motor for the Messerschmitt Me262 jet fighter.

MG

Produced: 1923–date.
The Badge: The MG badge is a back-to-back rendition of the letters set in a 1930s, fashionable art deco octagon of chocolate and cream colours.

William Morris, founder of Morris Motors (whose story is told elsewhere), owned a chain of retail premises under the name Morris Garages. The founder of the MG marque, Cecil Kimber, was appointed to run these in 1922. He developed sporting bodies for basic Morris models and named them after the initials of the Morris Garages chain, and MG was born.

His small production sports models would be called Midgets (small things), with different models being differentiated by using letters: A, B and C type, etc. They created a style famous even to this day. Larger cars would be labelled Magna ('big') and Magnette ('little Magna').

In the 1950s came the new generation MGs started by the MG-A, followed by the MG-B and larger engine MG-C in a simple evolution of a basic design.

The octagonal MG badge, seen here in the classic chocolate and cream colours, would be reproduced in a range of colours and styles over the years of MG production. Often as a simple chrome design allowing the body colour of the car to show through.

After a time being used simply as a badge of performance versions of Austin-Rovers cars, in 1995 the first new MG sports car for many years arrived as the MGF. (The MG-D and MG-E were prototypes that never made it into production.) It would, in turn, spawn the simpler MG TF, which resurrected another name from the past.

Mini

Produced: 1959–date.
The Badge: Early production Minis wore the badge they were marketed under (Austin models wore Austin badges, Morris versions wore Morris badges, and so on). Later models following rationalisation wore a simple upright shield on their grille with the word 'Mini' across the top. Much later a winged Mini symbol was adopted as a bonnet badge, and remains current to today.

On the last of the Rover Group cars and from then on to models made by BMW, this bold winged Mini badge was adopted.

The upright shield Mini badge was used from the time the range was rationalised in 1969 (previously Austin and Morris badges had been used) until the last Rover Group models.

The Mini was not originally known as simply Mini. When launched it was sold as both the Austin New Seven and the Morris Mini Minor, depending on which dealership chain sold it. The Austin name recalled the immensely successful pre-war Austin Seven range, while the Morris name referred to it being a smaller version of the popular Morris Minor. They were all christened 'the Mini' by enthusiasts, and when the range was rationalised in 1969 the Mini name was adopted for all models.

The Mini Cooper sporting model arose from a contract with rally driver John Cooper who had been tuning Minis with great success. His designs were put into production under licence using his name.

Mitsubishi

Produced: 1917–date.
The Badge: The company badge of three interlocked gemstones or diamonds is simply described as 'Mitsubishi' in Japanese. It is made up of the words 'Mitsu', which means 'three' and 'Hishi', which translates as 'water chestnuts'. In colloquial Japanese it is used to refer to any diamond or rhomboid shape and can be translated to mean 'three precious stones'.

The company was founded by Yataro Iwasaki and he chose this as his emblem. It is derived from the stacked squares of the Iwasaki family crest arranged as if they were water chestnuts and a tribute to the coat of arms of his financiers, the Tosa clan. In 1990, Mitsubishi would produce a cruise ship named *Crystal Harmony* in honour of the badge.

Mitsubishi's best-known product in Europe, the Shogun, was named after a historical Japanese warrior class. It was probably in the best interest of the Mitsubishi brand reputation that the Mitsubishi Lettuce never came to the UK.

The Mitsubishi badge represent the company name. A colloquial translation of Mitsubishi would be 'three precious stones'

Morgan

Produced: 1909–date.

The Badge: Very early Morgans had the model title written on a curved title under the winged Morgan legend stamped into their brass radiators.

Current Morgan badging practice has them wear a winged 'Morgan' badge with the model number given on a simple vertical bar running through the horizontal wording. The engine size (in cylinders) is usually below the word 'Morgan' and the model designation above.

Founded by H. F. S. Morgan, the cars that bore his name started out as three wheelers (Harrods was their first agent), but with two at the front rather than following the Reliant practice of a single wheel at the front. Four-wheeled cars came later.

Model designations tend to be a symbol followed by the number of engine cylinders (e.g. +4, +8) or sometimes number of seats followed by number of engine cylinder (e.g. 4/4)

The long-standing pattern Morgan badge lists the company names across the centre bar of the badge and the model number on the vertical bar. Here, the model is the +8, a V8 powered model.

Above: This last pattern badge to grace the Morris range as fitted to the Ital. The marque had fallen so far from grace at the British Leyland group that the marque name was not even used.

Left: The earliest pattern Morris badge shows the coat of arms of the city of Oxford (Oxenford, the Ox at the Ford., a ford in this case being a shallow crossing place in a river.) with company name above and the model beneath.

Morris

Produced: 1913–84.

The Badge: The original Morris badge was an Ox at the Ford, the symbol of the city of Oxford, with the Morris name written above and the model designation beneath. Later versions would move the word 'Morris' to beneath the coat of arms. This was adopted for the first production Morris that was called the Oxford. This name was chosen as the Morris factory was at Cowley, near Oxford.

The last Morris cars would lose their heraldic badge and be badged with a bland set of three blue lines before the Morris name was allowed to lapse.

William Morris (later Viscount Nuffield), as was common at the time, ran a garage before moving into car production and using his family name as a title for his new marque,

His first car would be the Oxford, followed by a larger Cowley, named after the village that actually housed the factory (Minis are made on the same site today) and the small Morris would become the Minor. There would also be a range-topping large model called Isis, named after the Egyptian goddess.

The original Oxford (the name would be reused many times) was known as 'Bull Nosed', short for bullet nosed, after the resemblance of the polished brass radiator to a rifle bullet.

The last Morris was the Ital saloon, named after the Italian Ital design studio that styled it.

Nissan

See under Datsun.

The simple Noble badge was very much a thing of it's time. Clear, bold and easy to read.

Noble

Produced: 1999–date.
The Badge: Noble cars wear a simple yellow rectangular badge with the marque name boldly within in black in a simple font. The company was formed by Lee Noble to produce high-performance cars designed by himself and that bear his name. Model names have all so far been numbers derived from engine horsepower outputs.

Packard

Produced: 1899–1958.
The Badge: Early Packards wore a red and gold embossed coat of arms of a knight's helmet surmounted by a pelican. This ornate coat of arms was that of the company founder's ancestor Samuel Packard, who had emigrated from Essex in England in seventeenth century.

Packard's Goddess of Speed mascot was likely either inspired by or designed to copy the Spirit of Ecstasy as used by Rolls-Royce.

This Packard Twelve (so named because of the V12 engine) clearly shows the shouldered grille for which all but the earliest models were recognisable.

During the 1920s Packards could be ordered with a Goddess of Speed bonnet mascot of a flying lady clutching a wheel in her outstretched hands, clearly inspired by, or even intended as a parody of, the Rolls-Royce flying lady.

Later Packards are recognised less by their badge (seldom used on later models) than by the shape of their radiator. These invariably had 'shoulders' on each top edge.

The Packard brothers James Ward and William gave their name to Packard cars when they put their coat of arms badge on a redesigned product of the recently purchased Winton car company.

Early models had letters, e.g. model A. Later there would be a Packard Twelve, the world's first production V12-engined car with an engine based on the Liberty aero engine, and Packard Sixteen, the first mass-produced V16 engine.

Peugeot

Produced: 1891–date.

The Badge: The Peugeot family ironmongery business originated in 1810, and one of their products was saw blades. The still current Lion badge of Peugeot cars was adopted as their logo as the symbol of strength and speed, which was felt to be the perfect attributes of a saw.

Peugeot's Lion was originally intended as a symbol of strength and speed where applied to a range of saw blades made before they entered the motoring business.

The head of the Peugeot family, Armand Peugeot, started production of cars as part of the family business. At one time there were two ranges of Peugeot cars being built by separate brothers: there was the original Peugeot brand and the Lion-Peugeot brand being produced at the same time. They were amalgamated in 1910.

Most Peugeot cars have been given numbers rather than names, always with a 'o' on the middle. This numbering system was created in 1936 and is still in use today.

The first number places the model within the range (i.e. models prefixed 2 are smaller than those prefixed 3) and the last number is the number of models in that range they have produced (i.e. the 205 was introduced before the 206, following on to production of the 207, etc.).

Plymouth

Produced: 1928–2000.
The Badge: The badge of Plymouth cars was of a sailing ship, a representation of the *Mayflower* landing the Pilgrims at Plymouth Rock, Massachusetts. As the value for money marque in the Chrysler corporation car range, the ship often sat above the legend 'Product of the Chrysler Corp USA'.

The name Plymouth was chosen for the new Chrysler marque by employee Joe Frazer. It was named after the popular Plymouth binder twine made by the local Plymouth

The sailing ship on the Plymouth badge was a representation of the *Mayflower* landing the Pilgrims on Plymouth Rock.

Cordage Company. It was a popular product with the local farmers, who were considered their target market. Both car and twine were initially manufactured in the town of Plymouth.

Pontiac

Produced: 1926–date.
The Badge: The original badge of the Pontiac car was of an Natrive American head, and some would wear bonnet mascots of the same inspiration.

When General Motors announced their new upmarket brand, it was to be based and manufactured in the town of Pontiac, Michigan. They named their new brand after the

The head of Native American Chief Pontiac was the symbol of the upmarket brand of the General Motors company. Very prominent on early models. It would slowly become less obvious over the years.

town. The town itself was named after an Ottawa Native American chief who caused the frontier to revolt against the British in 1763. The head of Chief Pontiac was chosen as the emblem of their new marque.

After a period of rationalisation by GM, Pontiac sat between Chevrolet and Cadillac in the GM family.

The best-known Pontiac remains the Trans-Am, named after a popular national racing series, for which GM had to pay a royalty for each one sold.

Porsche

Produced: 1940–date.

The Badge: The Porsche shield is derived from the town shield of Stuttgart, where Porsche was born, with the company name added across the top of the shield.

The Antlers to the top left and bottom right of the shield come from the crest of the counts of Württemberg, whose capital was Swabia, an old name for Stuttgart. The red and black stripes are taken from the flag of the region.

The horse in the centre of the shield was inspired by the riding school and stud for which Stuttgart is famous – Stuttgart translates to 'stud farm'.

The company was founded by engineer Ferdinand Porsche to produce his own designs. Previously he had worked for Styer, Austro-Daimler, Zundap and NSU. He had also produced such gifted designs under the Nazis as the Tiger tank and the VW Beetle.

The Porsche badge has changed little of the years, effectively being the coat of arms of the city of Stuttgart.

Most Porsche models used numbers rather than names, but two terms have become synonymous with Porsche cars. The first, Turbo (often written large along the side of the car), denotes their forced induction system that added to their engine power. It was coined when a turbo was an unusual fitment seen only on exotic cars. Today most modern cars come with them, but the association remains. The other is Carrera, a homage to Porsche's success in the Carrera Panamericana race in Mexico.

More recently names have been adopted for their large vehicles such as Macan (tiger), Cayenne (a hot pepper) and Cayman (a South American alligator).

Princess

Produced: 1947–82.
The Badge: Princess cars wore a red enamel royal crown atop their chrome radiator grilles. The cars themselves were styled with prominent chrome grilles long after they had ceased to be fashionable.

After the Second World War, Austin set their sights higher than their more usual family models. In 1947, the Sheerline and Princess ranges was launched aimed at the Rolls-Royce/ Daimler market. They were big, luxurious cars.

They were a sales failure and were soon renamed simply 'Princess' as a nod to their intended royal customers, starting a long line of vehicles that would live on into the 1980s. Built by the famous Vanden Plas coachbuilding company, they were always based on a regular Austin product with the Princess grille and Crown badge added to the front. Inside, the basic Austin interior was replaced with an ultra-traditional design with leather seats, picnic tables and a burr walnut dashboard.

One model, the 4-litre R, was powered by a Rolls-Royce engine, making it one of few cars outside the Rolls-Royce range to be allowed to officially wear their badge.

The simple red enamel crown would remain on upmarket British Leyland cars right up until 1982 when the Austin Allegro based version ceased production.

Proton

Produced: 1985–date.

The Badge: Early UK Protons wore a badge consisting of a ring of overlapping stars around the edge. There was one star for each of the Malaysian states, plus one for Malaysia itself. Local examples would have a simpler star with a point for every state and a Muslim crescent beneath.

When Proton took control of Lotus cars in the UK they created a new badge: a stylised tiger head within a green circle on the blue field of a heraldic shield shape. The new tiger's head insignia symbolised Malaysia's national heritage and is taken from the two tigers on the Malaysian national coat of arms. The tiger's head is set on a deep green circle that was taken from the Lotus badge to symbolise their future close-knit working relationship after they had purchased the company. The deep blue background of the shield was taken from the Malaysian flag.

Initially a joint venture between Mitsubishi and the Malaysian government, the name Proton was an abbreviation of Perusahaan Otomobil Nasional, which translates as 'National

Above left: The early style Proton badge for overseas markets has one star for each of the Malaysian states and one for Malaysia itself.

Above right: The later style Proton badge following their purchase of British Lotus incorporates the colours of the Malaysian flag and the national symbol of the tiger taken from their coat of arms. The green circle pays homage to Lotus and their future involvement in Proton cars.

69

Automobile Company'. Proton aimed to provide locally produced cars at sensible prices for the local population and was soon exporting them.

In 1996, Proton purchased British manufacturer Lotus and used their expertise in the field of vehicle dynamics to improve their vehicles. The first flowering of this partnership was the Satria ('knight'), which was considered the best Malaysian car made to that date. Other models have included the Persona ('person'), Wira ('hero' or 'man'), Putra ('son') and Juara ('champion').

Reliant

Produced: 1935–2001.
The Badge: Most Reliants were badged with a simple line of text on a shield. Three wheelers would have the name sitting above a chrome triangle to signify their famous three-wheeled designs. Later models would wear a stylised castle badge as a nod to Tamworth Castle, which was near the Reliant factory.

In 1934, Tom Williams purchased the rights to build the Raleigh Safety Seven delivery van. This was a three-wheeled van powered by an Austin Seven engine. Williams sought to develop the vehicle using parts that had come with his purchase of the production rights. As many of these parts were stamped with an 'R' when produced by Raleigh, he worked his way through the 'R' section of the dictionary until he found a word that he felt suited the ethos of his new vehicle. The most suitable word he could find was Reliant, and a marque was born.

The simple Reliant badge with a triangle-shaped lower section in homage to their fame for producing three-wheeled cars.

Best remembered today for their three wheelers, Reliant offered four-wheeled versions of all their small designs The three-wheeled Regal spawned four-wheeled Rebel, and the Robin led to four-wheeled Kitten. They also offered a range of sporting coupes and estates named after the swords Sabre and Scimitar.

A model supplied uniquely to the Israeli market was known as Sabra, which means 'a Jew born in Israel'.

Renault

Produced: 1898–date.

The Badge: The grille badge initially worn by Renault cars was an intricate design intertwining the initials of the Renault brothers in a geometric design.

In time, at one time or another, they would use a head on image of a motorcar within a gear wheel, a side on view of a military tank in a circle, and a circular design with the Renault name across the centre.

The stretched square symbol we see on Renaults today was initially used to provide an aperture for the horn to be sounded through. For cars without a grille, a simple stretched square symbol with Renault written across the centre was used.

The Renault marque was founded by the Renault brothers Louis, Marcel and Fernand to produce a range of the then newly invented cars for the French people.

Their first post-Second World War mass-produced saloon was the Dauphine (a French female feudal title), and their performance cars were named Gordini after the tuning company founded by Amédée Gordini that designed and manufactured them.

While far from being the only badge Renault have ever used, the current design was originally adopted to give an aperture through which a horn could be sounded.

Most famous of the Renault models was the Espace (space), which was a design Renault inherited from Matra when they took over the company. It was arguably the world's first people carrier in the sense we understand the term today.

Riley

Produced: 1899–1969.

The Badge: The Riley badge has 'Riley' in script in a blue diamond atop a hooded radiator grille. The exact shade of blue changed with time and sometimes denoted the state of tune or engine size of a model.

The Riley family led by Percy Riley purchased the Bonnick cycle company in 1890 as an investment and renamed their products as Rileys. Percy Riley personally took control of the company in 1912 when the other members of the family moved on to other enterprises.

Their sporting cars were named after famous racing circuits such as Brooklands (the world's first purpose-built racing circuit) and Le Mans. Later luxury saloons famous for their cloth roofs long after the fashion had passed would be christened the RM (Riley Motors) series followed by a letter denoting the engine size and order of production (i.e. the RMA was the first in the series and had the smallest engine, followed by the RMB, etc.).

Later models under the BMC umbrella were given names including Kestrel (a bird of prey), Pathfinder (named after a wartime RAF formation that went ahead of Bomber command to mark targets) and Elf (a small mythical creature, presumably chosen as it was a version of the Mini.).

The Riley badge was set atop a hooded radiator, seen here with the classic dark blue background. Smaller-engined models sometimes featured a light blue background to the badge.

Rolls-Royce

Produced: 1904–date.

The Badge: The company badge consists of the two Rs of the company founders' surnames intertwined and set above what is described as a Palladian grille. Where space permits, the legend 'Rolls' is written above the initials and 'Royce' beneath.

Early models had the lettering in red, changing to black in 1933. Some say it was changed because of the death of the engineer partner Royce, other sources claiming it was changed to fit in better with the fashions and colours of the time.

On top of the famous grille sits what is known as the 'Flying Lady' figurine, correctly described as 'the Spirit Ecstasy'. A standard sculpture adopted from the 1920s as an alternative to the often risqué mascots being fitted to Rolls-Royces by their owners. It was modelled for by Eleanor Velasco Thornton and sculpted by Charles Sykes. An early version was entitled the Whisperer as the figure had a finger to her lips, but it was soon revised to the famous figure still in use today. In the interests of modern health and safety rules current example are spring loaded and retract into the radiator grille when struck.

Henry Royce was an inspired engineer, and he joined forces with the Hon. Charles Rolls when he offered Royce a deal to buy every car he manufactured, badged as a Rolls-Royce in honour of their partnership. Strangely, there are no known pictures of the two men together.

The most famous Rolls-Royce is the Silver Ghost, but this was never an official model name. Silver Ghost was a specific 40/50 model owned by the factory and used for publicity purposes.

The intertwined twin Rs of Rolls-Royce and the Spirit of Ecstasy remain two of the best-known automotive insignias in the world. In the very early days the twin Rs were rendered in red.

Early models had names based on engine outputs while later models would have names chosen for their upmarket sound. The largest Rolls-Royce was always the Phantom while 'smaller' models were usually badged as Silver followed by a second word. There would be a Silver Dawn among others, but the Silver Mist name was proposed but never used as Mist had impolite connotations in German slang.

Rover

Produced: 1904–2005.

The Badge: Rover adopted the symbol of the Viking for their car range (previously the name had been used on their penny-farthing bicycles as far back as 1877 when the company was founded by J. K. Starley and W. Sutton) as they felt that the Vikings were the world's most successful 'Rovers' or wanderers.

Rover cars wore a depiction of a Viking longship in a number of increasingly stylised forms. Early versions had the word 'Rover' written on the ship's sails with the model number beneath while later badges had the word written above the depiction of the longship. Some Rovers displayed depictions of a bearded Viking's head as a mascot or within the chrome of the radiator grille.

From 2001 the newly independent Rover company added an enamel Union Jack flag badge in some form to all their models, and it would remain until production ceased in 2005.

Early Rovers were badged by engine power, while after the Second World War the 'P' (for 'post-war') ranges arrived. The P4 were famously known as 'Auntie' Rovers after a journalist described driving one as being like visiting a favourite aunt. The first of

Above: A classic rendition of the Viking longship badge with the model number beneath and a chrome Viking above.

Left: The highly simplified and stylised Viking longship badge as seen towards the end of the Rover line. The very last badges would omit the Rover name.

the P4 range featured a single centre-mounted spot light and would become informally known as the Cyclops Rover. Their early automatic gearboxes were marketed as 'Roverdrive'.

When Rover purchased the rights to build a 'small' 3.5-litre V8 from American Buick the suffix 'B' was added to the model designation to signify the V8 was fitted, i.e. the P5 became the P5B. The new V8 rejuvenated the Rover range and any car powered by the engine was immediately colloquially known as a Rover V8 no matter which range it was part of.

Later models would be badged with simple numbers, the first number indicating the car size (higher numbers were bigger cars) and the second two digits advised the engine size (e.g. a Rover 820 was an 800 series car with a 2-litre engine). High performance Rovers would be badged Vitesses (meaning 'fast').

SAAB

Produced: 1950–2014.

The Badge: Early SAAB products wore a head-on representation of an aeroplane (the main business of their parent company) above the company initials on their grille.

Later models adopted the crowned Griffin crest, symbol of the Skane district of Sweden where the Scania truck division of Saab was based. When SAAB merged with Scania trucks they adopted their badge and retained it until production ceased. The marque name 'SAAB' was written above the Griffin while Scania was written beneath.

The SAAB name stands for Svenska Aeroplan Aktie Bolaget, which translates as Swedish Aeroplane Company.

Model names were largely numbers, but there would be editions named after rally successes (Monte Carlo) and their famous racing drivers (Carlsson). There was also a small sports coupe named Sonnet, meaning a short piece of rhyming poetry.

Above left: The first SAAB car badges alluded the business of their parent company and used an aeroplane as part of their badge.

Above right: Following their merger with Skania trucks, the Griffin badge of the latter, the badge of Skane province of Sweden, would be adopted.

SEAT

Produced: 1950–date.

The Badge: SEAT cars are badged with a stylised 'S' representing the first letter of the company name.

Early models that were licence-built direct copies of FIAT models retained the depression on their bonnet or grille where the FIAT emblem had been mounted. On these cars a winged SEAT emblem was developed to exactly fill the mounting.

The SEAT name is created from the initials of the company name, Sociedad Española de Automóviles, which translates as Spanish Automobile Society. Initially a state-owned company set up to produce locally built cars for the Spanish market, it started out producing licensed-built copies of FIAT models with similar names. Then a whole family of lightly restyled versions were created named after Spanish tourist resorts. There was Marbella, Cordoba, Malaga and Ibiza.

Later models included Salsa (a Latin American dance and hot sauce), Alhambra (named after the palace of the Islamic kings of Granada), Toledo (named after the famous steel-producing Spanish city) and people carrier Altea (Greek for 'one who takes care').

The stylised 'S' of SEAT cars is derived from the fist initial of the company name.

Singer

Produced: 1905–70.

The Badge: Singer cars were badged by a simple 'Singer' legend within a decorative shield shape.

The company was founded by and named after George Singer. The original company went into receivership in 1908 and was reformed as Singer and Co. in 1909 following the death of the founder

By 1927 Singer was the third-largest producer of motor cars in the UK and, for reasons that remain obscure, had a huge following in Spain.

In 1955, Singer was purchased by the Rootes Group and joined Hillman, Sunbeam and Humber in their portfolio of marques.

The Singer Gazelle (a fast-moving kind of antelope) arrived in 1956. A larger version based on the larger Hillman Super Minx and called the Singer Vogue (meaning current fashion, and a name that would remain with Singer until their demise) joined the range in 1961. There would also be a Singer version of the Hillman Imp named Chamois after a small Antelope to fit in the range below the larger Gazelle.

Skoda

Produced: 1895–date.

The Badge: The Skoda badge is based on a flying arrow bonnet mascot that was used on Skoda cars during the 1930s. Popular legend has it that this was inspired by an Native American servant working in the household of one of the company founders, while other sources point to a painting of an Native American in the Skoda management office as the inspiration.

The story of the Skoda car began in 1895 when bookseller Vaclav Klement and bicycle mechanic Vaclav Laurin set up a factory in Mlada Boleslav near Prague (Skoda is still there today) in what was then Austro-Hungary and produced cars under the name Laurin-Klements.

In 1925, heavy industrial company and military manufacturer Skoda, founded by Emil Skoda, merged with Laurin-Klement. For a while the cars carried both Skoda and Laurin-Klement badges, but the original name was soon dropped in favour of Skoda.

The model names still being used today soon arrived. There was a Monte Carlo, named after their successes in the rally of the same name, a range-topping model named Superb and a sporting model called a Rapid.

Their eighth production model after the Second World War arrived in 1958 and was christened Octavia (number eight) alongside the Felicia (meaning 'happy').

Their first hatchback, and arguably first modern Skoda after their long-lived rear-engined Estelle (meaning 'star') range car, was the Favorit ('favourite') of 1989. In time the Skoda hatchback would become the Fabia (meaning 'fabulous'), while other model names became routinely reused by new owners Volkswagen from the company's history.

Their current sporting brand is VRS, which stands for 'Victory Racing Sport'.

Currently rendered entirely in chrome, the earlier version of the SMART car badge had the arrow on the right coloured yellow.

SMART

Produced: 1998–date.

The Badge: The original version of the badge was a silver 'C' on the left with a yellow arrow on the right followed by the marque name. The C stands for 'compact' and the yellow triangle is said to signify the forward-thinking nature of their designs. Later models have the whole design finished in silver.

The SMART brand came about through a joint venture between the Swatch Design brand and Mercedes cars. Known during design at Swatch as the Swatchmobile, Mercedes pushed for a more neutral name. An amalgam of the initials of Swatch, Mercedes, and the word ART were finally put together to form the brand SMART.

Their models are listed by numbers, the first being number of wheels, the second the number of seats, i.e. the SMART fourtwo has four wheels and two seats, the SMART fourfour has four wheels and four seats.

SS

Produced: 1927–940.

The Badge: SS Cars were badged with a simple Cyrillic SS in a pentagonal surround in chrome on their radiator grilles.

William Lyons founded what would become SS Cars in 1922, initially producing motorcycle sidecars under the Swallow (as in the bird) brand name. He christened his business Swallow Sidecars, which was abbreviated to simply SS for his production cars.

SS started by constructing coach-built bodies on existing manufacturers chassis frames, and would produce his first production model, an SS-bodied Austin Seven, known as the Austin Seven Swallow.

The Cyrillic SS initials used for William Lyon's first cars stood for Swallow Sidecars. After the Second World War the name had to be discarded following the use of the letters by Hitler's Nazi regime.

The year 1931 would see the launch of the sporty SS (Swallow Sports) 1, quickly followed by the smaller SS 2. A trend he would continue after the Second World War began with the SS 90 and SS 100 models, letters followed by a number that would denote the model's top speed. The most powerful models would be christened Jaguar after the fast-moving cat and be supplied with a suitable mascot.

Following the Second World War and the negative associations the German army had created for the initials SS, the whole range was renamed Jaguar for 1945.

Standard

Produced: 1903–63.

The Badge: The original Standard cars were badged with a winged Union Jack flag or British standard (a military flag) with the company name written across the top. Their location, Coventry, was written around the base of the badge.

During the 1950s models were badged with a heraldic-style shield shared with the Triumph range, with 'Standard' written around the bottom of the shield. Some versions were in blue and silver, some red.

Standard Motors was founded by R. W. Maudsley in 1906, and there are two versions of how Standard cars came by their name. One states that the company intended to make as many parts of possible interchangeable or 'standard' between their various models. Another school of thought says the company's founder wanted to suggest to their customers that all their products were 'of a standard', i.e. of better quality than those of the competition.

Early production cars were named after British tourist resorts such as Rhyl, Teignmouth and Stratford.

Their first post-war production car was the Vanguard (the foremost part of a military formation), soon joined by smaller saloons named after their nominal horsepower. These would go upmarket as the Pennant (a small naval flag), a rendition of which would appear on their badge.

The original Standard badge made use of a patriotic Union Jack flag and the location of the factory. Some cars would also display an ancient Roman military standard as a radiator mascot.

Much later, as part of Standard-Triumph this shield was adopted as the marque badge. The Standard name is written around the base of the shield and the colours were variously red and black or blue and black depending on the model.

Vanguard production ended in 1963, and the Standard name was dropped in the UK in favour of the more sporting Triumph name also owned by the company.

The Standard name would continue in India until 1988, making cars based on updated Triumph and Vauxhall designs.

Studebaker

Produced: 1904–67.

The Badge: Studebaker cars were badged initially with the 'rolling wheel' symbol of an early type of spoked wagon wheel with the legend 'Studebaker' written across it in handwritten script. This was inspired by their earlier, pre-motoring products. At one time they operated the largest wagon factory in the world.

There would also be a bonnet (or radiator cap) mascot in the form of a figure leaning forwards, with one arm outstretched known as Atalanta, named after a virgin huntress of Greek mythology.

The marque was founded in South Bend, Indiana, by the Studebaker brothers Henry and Clem, the official title of the company being the Studebaker Brothers Manufacturing Company. They would make electric as well as petrol-powered cars at various times, their business finally folding after an ill-fated merger with Packard.

The Studebaker wheel badge harks back to the days when the Studebaker brothers owned one of the largest wagon manufacturing plants in the world. The mascot is Atalanta, a figure from Greek mythology.

The UK would see a handful of Studebakers arrive with the US forces during the Second World War in the form of the militarily named Commander. Twelve were imported, of which at least one still exists. Their Avanti (meaning 'forward') sports car would live on long after the company folded, passing through a number of hands before production ended.

Subaru

Produced: 1956–date.

The Badge: Subaru is the Japanese name for a group of stars in the Pleiades constellation, of which six are visible to the naked eye. It is often referred to in ancient Chinese and Japanese literature and is considered a lucky omen.

Their first president, Kenji Kita, has been quoted as saying that Japanese cars should have Japanese names, so he chose the name Subaru for their first production vehicle.

As Fuji Heavy Industries (the parent company of Subaru) had been created by amalgamating six smaller companies, it seemed to ideal choice to name their first car, and it would go on to become the name of their whole passenger vehicle line. The word can also be translated as meaning 'to gather together'.

Their best-known model name is Impretza, or 'impressive', for their successful rally car range.

The six stars in the Subaru badge are a representation of stars in the Taurus or Pleiades constellation. They are a traditional Japanese good luck symbol and also represent the companies brought together to form Subaru.

Sunbeam

Produced: 1901–76.

The Badge: Early Sunbeams were badged with a design of the sun bursting through the clouds with prominent sunbeams. In 1920, Sunbeam merged with Talbot/Darracq to form S. T. D. Motors Ltd (Sunbeam, Talbot, Darracq) and the Sunbeam badge became a script 'Sunbeam' word against an embossed background.

Following bankruptcy, the Rootes Group acquired the company in 1935 and amalgamated the Sunbeam name with that of the equally sporting Talbot marque, and Sunbeam-Talbot was formed. The family crest of the Earl of Shrewsbury and Talbot was retained as the new marque badge and would remain so until the end of production of cars bearing the Sunbeam name, long after the Talbot part of the name had been discarded.

The crest was centered around a Talbot hunting hound with a lolling tongue surmounted by a royal crown. The legend 'Rootes Group' was later added to the bottom of the badge.

There are many competing theories as to where the Sunbeam name originated from. It was adopted when company founder John Marston founded the Sunbeamland cycle factory. One theory suggests that it was inspired by a line in a hymn that ran 'Sunbeams scorching all the day', scorching being a slang term of the time for driving fast. Another is that it was named after the yacht used by Lord and Lady Brassey in their round the world voyage.

The Sunbeam Alpine was named after successes in the Alpine Rally, and saloon Rapier was named after a long, thin sword. The small Sunbeam based on the Hillman Imp would be named Stilleto, a smaller blade than a rapier.

Seen here in the original Talbot form, what would become the Sunbeam badge under the Rootes Group is derived from the coat of arms of the Earl of Shrewsbury and Talbot.

During the 1930s there was a Sunbeam Tiger world land speed record car, a name resurrected during the 1960s on an American V8-powered version of the Alpine sports car.

Sunbeam became a model as opposed to a marque name when Chrysler took control of the Rootes Group. It would become the Chrysler Sunbeam, a small hatchback. Unexpectedly, Sunbeam's last gasp of glory would come with the Chrysler (later Talbot) Sunbeam Lotus. The Lotus suffix denoted the fitting of the powerful Lotus 2.2-litre engine into the small hatchback to offer an incredible power to weight ratio and performance to match. It took the Sunbeam hatchback to first place in the World Rally championship in 1980.

Other parts of Sunbeam would produce buses and aero engines named after the people of the British Empire. Pathan and Sikh were buses, while Zulu and Afridi (among many others) were aero engines.

Suzuki

Produced: 1937–date.
The Badge: The Suzuki badge is a stylised 'S', signifying the first letter of the marque name.

The company that gave birth to Suzuki cars (and motorcyles) was formed in 1909 by Michio Suzuki for the design and production of weaving looms. Over the years Suzuki have moved into a huge range of commercial areas.

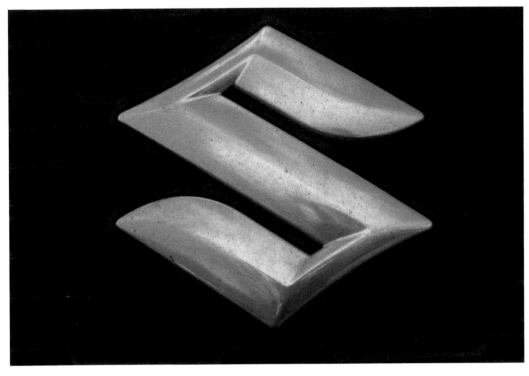

The simple 'S' of the Suzuki badge is derived from the initial letter of the company name.

Model names have included Baleno (a sudden and brief flash of light or energy), Swift (fast moving), Jimney (allegedly originally to be named a Jimmy after a trip by executives to Scotland, but that got misspelled somewhere along the line), and Vitara ('life is good').

Toyota

Produced: 1936–date.
The Badge: The Toyota badge is a lucky symbol of three interlocked rings in the shape of a 'T' for Toyota. The rings represent the heart of the customer, the heart of the product and the boundless opportunities ahead.

Sakichi Toyoda sold a weaving loom patent in the UK in 1929 that produced the capital required for his son Kiichiro to found the car manufacturer we know today.

In 1937, the Toyota spelling of the family name was adopted as it was it was considered easier for foreign language to pronounce and spell. Some sources suggest that as Toyota only needed eight characters to write in Japanese, and Toyoda took ten, it was changed as it was considered luckier in Japan to have a company name with eight characters.

Their first mass-produced car was the Corona (crown). A factory was later set up in the UK to access European markets and initially produced the Carina E, the 'E' standing for European.

Their large four-wheel-drive vehicles derived their name from the likes of Land Rover and was christened Land Cruiser.

The three rings of the Toyota badge are said to represent the heart of the company, the heart of the customer and the boundless opportunities ahead.

The stark 'S' badge of Trabant cars was inspired by the Sputnik satellite, which was launched at the same time as the car.

Trabant

Produced: 1959–90.
The Badge: All Trabant cars have a capital 'S' badge in an oval setting.

The name Trabant is derived from the old German word 'drabant', which translates as 'satellite' or 'companion'. This is often used in astronomical circles to describe a moon. The name of the car was inspired by the then current Russian Sputnik (which means companion or fellow traveller) satellite, hence the capital 'S' badge was adopted.

To keep costs and weight down, the body of the Trabant was not made of metal but of something called Duraplast. This was a compound of cotton waste and Phenol resins, which proved remarkably durable. At the end of their working lives and following the fall of the Berlin Wall, disposal became a major problem for the reunited Germany.

Produced largely without changes for the whole of its life, Trabant was both marque and model name, providing basic transport for the citizens of the former East Germany and the adjoining parts of the USSR.

Triumph

Produced: 1923–84.
The Badge: Early Triumph cars wore a 3D globe insignia in a range of locations. It was chosen as symbolising their position as a marque known all over the world, their map of the world being unusually centered over central Europe with Great Britain on the top left.

On very early examples the British Empire was coloured in red in the atlas tradition of the time. This was dropped later and the entire land mass was coloured red against a blue sea.

An upright Standard-Triumph shield was used during the 1950s with the Triumph name written around the base. Sometimes in red and black, sometimes blue.

The final Triumphs wore a simple sans-serif 'Triumph' legend surrounded by a winner's garland badge to commemorate the victories of the Triumph Dolomite Sprint and TR7 V8 rally cars.

Right: The original Triumph globe badge was chosen to represent their position as a world marque. Strangely centred with England on the top left, a very early version had the British Empire coloured in red.

Below: The last Triumph badge was a simple 2D affair, the winners garland being added in commemoration of the racing successes of the TR7 V8 and Dolomite Sprint cars.

The Triumph company was founded in 1885 by German Siegfried Bettmann. He imported then started production of bicycles under the Triumph name, which he felt would would be easily recognisable and pronounceable in in any language.

The Gloria ('glorious') of 1933 would make Triumph famous, the fastest model being named Vitesse (meaning 'speed' or 'fast'). Later would come Dolomites, named after the Italian mountain range. Both names would be used again during the 1970s.

Immediately after the Second World War, Triumph produced a slightly dated touring convertible called the Triumph Roadster. Only a moderate success, the initials would live on in the successful range of sports cars that would succeed it in 1953, starting with the TR (Triumph Roadster) 2.The series would last until the TR8 of 1981.

The Triumph Herald saloon was named after a boat owned by a company director, and the Herald design would go on to be built for many years in India after production in the UK had ceased as the Standard Gazelle.

The Triumph name was used on the first of many Rover/Honda joint projects in the form of the reliable if uninspiring Acclaim (meaning to be praised enthusiastically and publicly). Production ceased in 1984 and the Triumph name ceased with it. Currently the name resides with BMW, following their ownership of what would become the Rover Group.

TVR

Produced: 1949–2012.

The Badge: All TVRs are badged in some form with the company initials. Early models wore them intertwined with ornate wings above within a triangular badge, while later models adopted modern, square letters, often in the form of decals rather than 3D badges.

The early TVR badge adopted the traditional winged rendition of the company name within an exuberant triangle.

Later TVR cars used a harder, square lettering style in the fashion of the time. Later models would keep this badge style but would display it as a simple decal.

Trevor Wilkinson originally set up Trevcar Motors to manufacture specials to specific customer requirements. He named the company after an abbreviation of his Christian name. When full series car production started under the TVR name Trevor became TreVoR, the capital letters becoming the name of TVR engineering and later TVR cars.

Cars headed for the USA would be named after their importer Jomar while the Grantura would be named after the company that supplied the fibreglass bodyshells.

The first TVR to wear the Griffith name were named after American dealer Jack Griffiths who would import TVRs less engines and fit them with large American V8 engines for his home market.

Among later models would be Vixen (colloquially a mischievous woman, more correctly a female fox) and Tamsin (a girl's name derived from the Old English word for 'twins'), Chimaera (a fire-breathing monster) and Cerbera (a three-headed beast of Greek legend).

Vauxhall

Produced: 1903–date.
The Badge: Vauxhall cars wear a Griffin badge, the one-time standard of Faukes de Breaute. Their first factory, then still known as Vauxhall Ironworks after their location, was in the Vauxhall area of London so his symbol was adopted.

The name of the area is derived from the term 'Vaux's Manor', the latter being the old English word for a hall. Vaux was Faukes de Breaute, who built his manor in the area in the thirteenth century. London slang still refers to an area a person is from as being their 'manor'.

The Vauxhall badge, seen here in full detail and colour, was originally a heraldic device used by Faukes de Breaute. He was Vaux, and the 'hall' part of the name was derived from the old English term for his manor. His influence would also give the name and insignia to the area of London.

The local council still uses the Griffin symbol, and it can be seen in the ironwork of Vauxhall Bridge crossing the Thames. When the company moved their factory to Luton, the word Luton was added to the lower edge of the badge.

American General Motors took control of Vauxhall in 1925, and post-Second World War their American influence would be very noticeable in the styling of their cars. There would be Wyvern (named after a dragon, likely inspired by the Griffin on the company badge), Cresta ('summit') and Velox ('fast' or 'rapid').

The year 1963 would see the arrival of their longest-running model name in the form of Viva, meaning 'alive' or 'full of cheer'. Production would run until 1979, then be resurrected again in the twenty-first century.

The famous high-performance Vauxhall Prince Henry produced immediately prior to the First World War was named in honour of Prince Henry of Prussia.

Vauxhall's commercial vehicle marque would be named after the neighbouring city of Bedford before eventually being dropped in favour of all their vehicles sharing the Vauxhall name.

Volkswagen

Produced: 1936–date.

The Badge: The Volkswagen badge is a simple representation of the initial letters of the company name displayed one above the other.

The Volks Wagen (correctly two words, VW hereafter) started life as an Adolf Hitler-sponsored scheme to manufacture a 1,000 Reichmark car for the German people to use on the new Autobahns. The title Volks Wagen literally translates as 'people's car'.

The VW (later christened Beetle after the shape) was initially known as the KDF (Kraft durch Freude) Wagon or 'Strength Through Joy' car, named after a Nazi leisure organisation.

A new town was constructed around the dedicated factory named Kraft durch Freude stadt or 'Strength Through Joy Town' (sometimes given as Stadt des KDF-wagens bei Fallersleben or city of the KDF car in Fallersleben). The frontispiece of the early Kraft durch Freude wagen brochures would show what would become the Beetle in front of a cogwheel design surrounding the Nazi Swastika. These brochures were a glorious full-colour design showing cross-sections of the car on layered clear plastic sheets, each printed with a different section of the car.

After the Second World War Kraft durch Freude stadt would be renamed Wolfsberg and early Beetles would wear the town crest on the centre of their steering wheels.

The simple 'V' and 'W' above one another stand for 'Volks Wagen' (technically two words) and this translates as 'People's Car'.

The cover of the first Beetle brochure clearly show its initial financiers. Hitler and the Nazi party intended the Beetle to be available for 1,000 Reichmarks to allow the German people of the name to use his new Autobahns.

Volvo

Produced: 1927–date.
The Badge: The Volvo badge is the symbol for iron, derived from the material they used for their original products, bearings.

Engineers Assar Gabrielsson and Gustav Larson took it upon themselves to design a car suited to the harsh Scandinavian conditions. Gabrielsson was the sales manager of the Swedish-bearing company SKF and was allowed to use of one of their registered trademarks for his project, AB Volvo. The name had originally been used by a subsidiary company that produced ball bearings – hence the marque name, Volvo, which is Latin for 'it rolls'.

Until recently Volvo models were given three-digit numbers: the first was the series number, the second the number of cylinders, the last the number of doors (including the hatchback on an estate). Later Volvos used a letter prefix to denote the model style and a number that denoted the size of the model. S stands for Sedan (Saloon), C for Coupe or convertible and V for versatile such as hatchbacks or SUVs. The larger the number following the letter, the larger the car.

The Volvo badge is the chemical symbol of iron, and the name simply translates as 'it rolls', derived from the fact the company initially made ball bearings.

Wartburg

Produced: 1898–1991.
The Badge: Wartburg cars were badged with a calligraphic-style rendition of the company name with an exaggerated flourish over the word.

Seen here from an early sales brochure, the Wartburg badge was a glorious colour design celebrating the Eisenacher motor works and the castle above the town that would supply both marque and model names.

An enamel nose badge was worn of a colourful art deco rendition of the silhouette of the castle above the town with the factory name 'Automobilwerk Eisenach' written across it.

The marque was named after Wartburg Castle, as depicted in the badge, which overlooks the town of Eisenach where the factory is based. The very first cars to be produced were referred to as Wartburgwagens, but the cars are best known for bearing the name Wartburg, which emerged after the partition of Germany. They were famous for being powered by a two-stroke, three-cylinder engines with only seven moving parts.

The Eisenach factory would also become home to the EMW and others until the factory was taken over by Opel and production of all the above was halted in favour of more modern designs.

Most Wartburgs had number model designations, but in some markets they were known as Warburg Knights, a name inspired by the historical occupants of the castle.

Wolseley

Produced: 1896–1975.
The Badge: Wolseley cars were badged with a raised shield displaying the Wolseley name in an ornate font surrounded by decorative knotwork surmounted by a pair of wings.

From 1933 this badge was mounted within the radiator grille on the central upright spar. Famously, it was illuminated when the car's lights were in use.

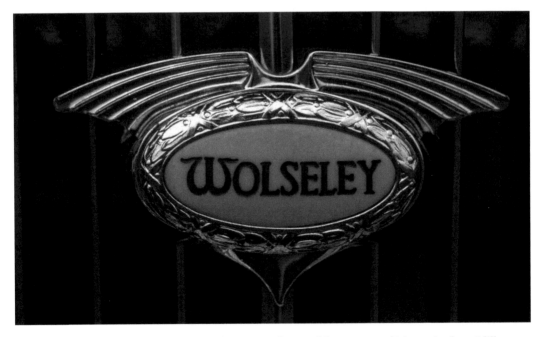

The Wolseley badge was made famous when it was designed from 1933 to light up in the middle of the radiator grille when the vehicle's lights were in use. This feature would stay with the marque until the end.

Wolseley cars were named after their parent company, the Wolseley sheep-sheering company of Australia (owned by Herbert Austin), with some involvement from the Vickers armaments company and engineer Hiram Maxim of machine-gun fame. The first car to bear the Wolseley name was designed by Herbert Austin, who would go on to create a marque and company under his own name.

Austin left in 1905 and for a brief period the cars were known as Wolseley-Siddeleys. Siddeley moved on in 1910 to start production of his own Siddeley-Deasey models and the cars were then badged simply as Wolseleys.

In 1930, Wolseley launched their most famous car: the Hornet, named after a form of wasp. Based on the 1930s Morris Minor, the name would be resurrected in 1961 attached to an upmarket version of the Mini.

Post-Second World War Wolseleys became largely badge-engineered versions of Morris models (their new owners) with uprated MG-derived engines (also part of the Morris group). They were adopted by the police in large numbers and were usually badged with a double number such as 16/60. The first number was the engine capacity, the second the horsepower produced.

The Wolseley name died quietly in 1975 as a purely badge-engineered version of the wedge-shaped Austin Princess range known simply as the Wolseley Saloon.

Acknowledgements

The author would like to thank the following people/organisations for permission to use copyright material in this book: Lada cars, Autovaz, Togliatti for permission to use an image of their logo, and Nissan Motor Manufacturing UK for permission to use an image from one of their early brochures.

Every attempt has been made to seek permission for copyright material used in this book. However, if I have inadvertently used copyright material without permission/ acknowledgement I apologise and will make the necessary correction at the first opportunity.